T0330779

Automation, Capitalism and the End of the Middle Class

In this book, the author argues that a new form of capitalism is emerging at the threshold of the Fourth Industrial Revolution. He asserts that we are in the midst of a transition from democratic capitalism to feudal capitalism and highlights how robotization and innovation is leading to a social crisis for the middle classes as economic inequality is on the rise.

Johannessen outlines the three elements – Balkanization, the Great Illusion, and the plutocracy – which are referred to here as feudal structures. He describes, analyzes, and discusses these elements both individually and in interaction with each other, and asks: "What structures and processes are promoting and boosting feudal capitalism?" Additionally, the book serves to generate knowledge about how the middle class will develop in the Fourth Industrial Revolution. It shows the various effects of robotization on the middle class, where middle class jobs are transformed, deconstructed, and re-constructed and new part-time jobs are created for the middle class.

Given the interest in the Fourth Industrial Revolution, the book will appeal to students of economic sociology and political economy as well as those in innovation and knowledge management courses focusing upon the emerging innovation economy. The topic will attract policymakers, and the accessible and engaging tone will also make the book of interest to the general public.

Jon-Arild Johannessen holds a Master of Science from Oslo University in History and a Ph.D. from Stockholm University in Systemic Thinking. He is currently professor (full) in Leadership at Kristiania University College, Oslo, and Nord University, Norway. He has been professor (full) in Innovation at Syd-Danske University, Denmark, and professor (full) in Management at The Arctic University, Norway. At Bodø Graduate School of Business, Norway, he had a professorship (full) in Information Management, and he has also been a professor in Knowledge Management at the Norwegian School of Management.

Routledge Focus on Economics and Finance

The fields of economics are constantly expanding and evolving. This growth presents challenges for readers trying to keep up with the latest important insights. Routledge Focus on Economics and Finance presents short books on the latest big topics, linking in with the most cutting-edge economics research.

Individually, each title in the series provides coverage of a key academic topic, whilst collectively the series forms a comprehensive collection across the whole spectrum of economics.

For a full list of titles in this series, please visit: www.routledge.com/Routledge-Focus-on-Economics-and-Finance/book-series/RFEF

Automation, Capitalism and the End of the Middle Class

Jon-Arild Johannessen

Routledge
Taylor & Francis Group

LONDON AND NEW YORK

First published 2019
by Routledge
2 Park Square, Milton Park, Abingdon, Oxon OX14 4RN

and by Routledge
52 Vanderbilt Avenue, New York, NY 10017

Routledge is an imprint of the Taylor & Francis Group, an informa business

© 2019 Jon-Arild Johannessen

British Library Cataloguing-in-Publication Data
A catalogue record for this book is available from the British Library

Library of Congress Cataloging-in-Publication Data
A catalog record for this book has been requested

ISBN: 978-0-367-25724-8 (hbk)
ISBN: 978-0-429-28941-5 (ebk)

Typeset in Times New Roman
by Apex CoVantage, LLC

Contents

Figures

Preface

This book builds upon the proposition that robots destroy hierarchies and bureaucracy.

Those who hold positions in private and public systems to a great deal constitute the middle class. These people have to a large degree had steering, control, and communication as their main activities in systems. Robots and informats will to a large degree take over all these activities. This will destroy bureaucracy and hierarchies. The hierarchies fade away, but the power to control will remain.

Prologue

Financial capital and bank executive boards around the world operate according to two considerations: profit and technological innovation. Banks are just going through a transition from classical banks to technological institutions. When Mason (2015: xiii) says that capitalism has reached a point after which it can no longer survive because it cannot adapt to the changes taking place currently, he is underestimating the logic of capitalism.

One of Mason's assumptions is that capitalism does not need democracy to survive. Capitalism may spawn a mutation that will allow a new form of capitalism to emerge. Of course, this has happened before: consider trade capitalism, industrial capitalism, information capitalism, and so on. In this book, we use the term 'feudal capitalism' to refer to the new form of capitalism that is emerging at the threshold of the Fourth Industrial Revolution.

Feudal structures existed for approximately 1,000 years throughout the Middle Ages. There is nothing to suggest that feudal capitalism could not function for another 1,000 years. Quite contrary to what Mason claims, capitalism has not evolved into post-capitalism or late capitalism, and it is not struggling to survive. Capitalism is not sick as social democrats say. Capitalism has never been as fresh and healthy as now.

Capitalism is flourishing in the area of tension between stability and change. It is not for nothing that conservative theoreticians say that we must change to maintain stability. This is precisely an insight from conservative thinkers, that change is essential for stability, not a threat against conservative values.

In the transition to feudal capitalism, it might be figuratively said that industrial capitalism in the global economy is the larva that has transformed into a butterfly and spread its wings. The fact that the butterfly has feudal structures is something few of the commonalty react to, because feudal capitalism ensures security and stability for the masses, takes care of their children's future, fulfils expectations, and solves security problems, diminishing possible terrorist attacks. There are only a few who are deeply worried about the fact that this has been done by neglecting democratic and humanist principles, because their daily lives have been stabilized and clarified. To understand what feudal capitalism may look like, one can look to China, and the power of Xi Jinping and the lords and peasants in his power structure.

Profit is given a new face: Janus' gentle face. However, in this context, Janus' harsh face is one representing inequality, showing the new precariat and working poor. The harsh face of feudal capitalism is presented as a necessary condition for the safety and security of the majority.

The new face of feudal capitalism shows itself as effective state government without the rhetoric and breach of promises of politicians. This new effective system of government is led by a group of technocratic experts, a type of bank executive board. This board delivers profits for financial capital and the well-off elite, as well as the 1% who benefit from economic growth through robotization and an extreme underpayment of the working poor. Feudal capitalism will create a new ideology in which government by experts and bank executive boards will be presented as the new rationality that 'everyone' profits from. However, the truth is rather that this serves the interests of the few, while the majority have to serve the few; the majority thus become the servants of the new feudal upper classes.

It is most probable that rationality and effectiveness, as well as the eradication of poverty, will be used as arguments in favour of feudal capitalism. Technological innovation will become the new religion because it is presented as a solution to the environmental crisis, the poverty crisis, and the great disparity between rich and poor. The ideas that have brought humanity to the threshold of its own destruction will be presented as the ideas that will bring humanity out of those crises. Capitalism's ideology will adapt perfectly to feudal capitalism, and democracy will be accused of being the main cause of the crises we find ourselves in.

If this analysis is correct, then we will enter a period where feudal capitalism governs through bank executive boards, possibly with a democratic appearance to create an impression of popular participation. However, in reality feudal capitalism will be just the next stage in the evolution of global financial capital.

This development by no means signals the end of capitalism, rather the end of a democratization process that has become too troublesome for capitalism. The effectiveness of feudal capitalism will be promoted by most people because more and more people will be drawn into prosperity, even though this will be at the expense of democratic processes. The mantra may quickly become that bread is more important than the free word.

While classic capitalism and the bourgeoisie have monopolized the concept of freedom, feudal capitalism will come to monopolize the idea of 'bread and work to the people' through effectiveness and innovation.

The left side of the political spectrum stood on the sidelines watching while the right side became the spokesman for 'freedom.' They will also come to stand on the sidelines again when 'bread and work to the people' becomes the right-wing mantra. It is not capitalism that has collapsed but rather the political left that has failed to adapt to global capitalism, thus becoming a historical footnote in people's consciousness because they are unable to deliver concrete proposals in changing times.

Feudal capitalism will be presented as something for the people, for the poor, for the outlying districts, for those who need the hope of a better future. However, despite being presented in this light, differences will nevertheless increase. The rich will become richer. Wage earners, project workers, and the new precariat will only get the crumbs from the table of the rich to compensate for lives that have become meaningless and characterized by a loss of mastery over their lives. The middle class will be eroded, crushed by the iron law of rationality, the robots, informats, and artificial intelligence, and their children will become the new service workers for the upper classes.

Just as in the Middle Ages, when the serfs had to pay homage to their lords, wage earners will also have to pay homage to their 'lords': the rich and the leaders of feudal capitalism. The left-wing mantra should perhaps be that we can no longer afford to feed and subsidize the rich.

While the class of industrial workers led the political left who fought for reforms through the Second and Third Industrial Revolutions, there are many indications that it will be groups of knowledge workers who will fight for change during the Fourth Industrial Revolution. They are educated; they are linked to the international information structure and know how the unequal distribution of resources is only increasing in feudal capitalism. This new class of knowledge workers will, in all likelihood, not support a left-wing solution of the kind we witnessed in Russia, China, and Cuba. The new left wing is anti-authoritarian, tends towards anarchist ideas, and is extremely freedom focused. The emerging creative class will no longer support the rich. They will be active in changing laws, regulations, and norms that allow tax havens, tax evasion, and so on.

The new knowledge class may be understood as being in rebellion against the 1% economy, where the few feed off the many. Possibly the next left-wing revolt will not emerge from a poor working class but from a pressed, declassed, and poorly paid middle class (Castells, 2013; Mason, 2015: xvii).

What seems to distinguish knowledge workers as a class is that they no longer tolerate social hierarchies with their governance and command structures. It is a globally linked class, which cannot be ruled by ideas of traditional obedience and loyalty structures (Castells, 2013). Mason clearly shows what powers the left-wing face when he quotes economists at the bank JPMorgan: "For neoliberalism to survive, democracy must fade" (Morgan, 2015: xx). The economists at JPMorgan are right and wrong at the same time. Neoliberalism will not survive, but it will transform into feudal capitalism. They are right when they argue that democracy will be eroded and transformed into governance by effective technocratic bank executive boards. Democracy will be replaced by people just like the economists of JP Morgan, and most people will be ruled by directives from bank executive boards in some form of disguise.

Introduction

To continue with the metaphor of capitalism as a living being, capitalism does more than adapt to change and learn from its mistakes. Capitalism also mutates and becomes something that is qualitatively new. This is the case concerning the Chinese economy. Western capitalists are investing in and reaping huge returns from production in China. China is a communist society with a government headed by the Communist Party. Western capitalists are hailing China, and China's communist leaders are hailing the Western investors (Gaskarth, 2015). The system that is emerging can be described as a form of feudal capitalism. China is governed without any democratic balancing mechanisms, while privately owned capital profits from its investments. This is a mutation of capitalism that is causing capitalism to adapt to communist operating conditions. It is also possible that this type of capitalist mutation could develop in Europe or the United States (though not under communist governments) with a form of feudal capitalism where technocrats and bureaucrats in, for example, the European Commission impose a framework of operating conditions. In practice, this situation would be like a board of bank directors controlling the development of the EU. This is a democratic scenario but with a system of government that is more reminiscent of a feudal overlord in charge of various niche areas.

What does it mean when we say that we are entering a new era where feudal capitalism affects most areas of our lives? Almost everyone will agree that capitalism has adapted throughout the ages, first from trade capitalism to industrial capitalism, and to information and knowledge capitalism. Change is taking place at the moment: capitalism is shedding its old skin and replenishing itself with the new skin of feudal capitalism to adapt to a new global era. Feudal capitalism is nourished by feudal structures – in other words, a whole new context of forms that figuratively resemble structures of the Middle Ages. This concerns ethics, ceremonies, rituals, and the formation of meaning. In the feudal structures of the Middle Ages, the nobles paid homage and pledged allegiance to the king. The king and the nobles had clear divisions of power that facilitated the maintenance and expansion of their power. However, the opportunities for the subjects of the king and the nobles (lords) were very limited, as they were hemmed in by fixed structures. How is the above description of feudal structures figuratively appropriate when discussing feudal capitalism? When Naomi Klein published

The Shock Doctrine in 2007, changes in capitalism were already evident. She describes how capitalism has begun to invoice and grossly profit on chaos. And not only that – capitalism creates chaos so as to profit from it. The best example is Iraq. The United States and their allies invaded, crushed, and made great efforts to rebuild the country. Super-profit and chaos appear to be a pattern in feudal capitalism. From Chile in 1973 to Iraq in 2003, chaos and super-profit have been an underlying pattern. In other words, this relationship between chaos and profit has manifested itself as the dominant doctrine of feudal capitalism. The economic crisis of 2007–2008 was also staged not by the few but by a system that needed to cleanse itself. Out of the crisis, super-profits were made by the few – the very few, the 1% who profit from chaos and crisis. This is the background of feudal capitalism. Naomi Klein writes as follows:

> Believers in the shock doctrine are convinced that only a great rupture – a flood, a war, a terrorist attack – can generate the kind of vast, clean canvases they crave. It is in these malleable moments, when we are psychologically unmoored and physically uprooted, that these artists of the real plunge in their hands and begin their work of remaking the world.
>
> (Klein, 2007: 21)

We have visualized the introduction in Figure 0.1, which also shows how the rest of the book is organized.

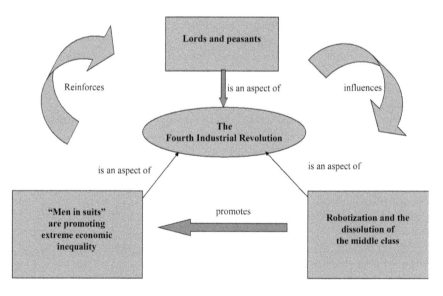

Figure 0.1 Feudal capitalism and the Fourth Industrial Revolution

1 Lords and peasants in the Fourth Industrial Revolution

Introduction

In this chapter, we have chosen to focus on three topics: Balkanization, the Great Illusion, and the plutocracy.

There are clear signs of trends that represent threats to democracy. Here we note the Balkanization of the democratic processes. The Balkanization of democracy did not start in 2007 with the financial crisis. The financial crisis merely uncovered trends that were already in existence. What is happening can be expressed in a single sentence: profit is being prioritized over the welfare of the general population.

The Great Illusion is described here as the idea that the free market improves universal welfare. However, there is no empirical research that can demonstrate this relationship. Although many hypotheses have been proposed about such a relationship, as well as considerable associated ideology, there is no evidence to support such a claim (Bauman, 2013; Chomsky, 2016a; Stiglitz, 2013, 2016). Most people seem unclear and unaware about the social mechanisms and the relationships between them that are relevant in this context. It is reasonable to assume that it is this absence of insight into both these social mechanisms and the related relationships that enables the plutocracy to grow and widen its reach almost unhindered.

The plutocracy (government by the wealthy) has grown in strength in step with a sharp increase in economic inequality (Stiglitz, 2013, 2016; Piketty, 2014, 2016). According to Bauman (2013), 1% of the population controls the major share of value creation. This conflicts with classical economic theory and the basic ideas underlying capitalism (Freeland, 2013: xii). Theoretically, inequality should decrease as incomes rise (Kuznets curve). This has not happened, however, and the world now has a new ruling class comprising the super-wealthy.

Balkanization

In this chapter, we use the term 'Balkanization' to refer to the fact that democracy, as we know it in the West, is under pressure (Chomsky, 2016: 2–4). It is under pressure from extreme centrists: those who always argue in favour of the free market and the free movement of capital. The efforts of the extreme centrists contribute to the international free flow of capital.

The crisis that was triggered in 2007 and which continues to reverberate around the world may be related to this free flow of capital. The crisis was caused by the so-called sub-prime loans in the American housing market. But how could the American housing market affect Europe, including public authorities in small local communities around Europe? Quite simply, the banks in America had sold their loans through complex financial instruments to local authorities and public sector bodies throughout Europe. When the bubble burst in the United States, it also burst in Europe (Macdonald, 2012: 37–69). Often, but not always, these financial instruments were divided into blocks or derivatives that could be freely distributed worldwide. These various derivatives were then sold as small units to creditors around the world. This kind of derivative block (pool) might be composed of several thousand original borrowers (Macdonald, 2012: 55). No matter how complex this situation was, it was *not* the basis of the crisis, merely the triggering factor. The basic cause was more deep-rooted and was basically the prioritization of profit over people (Chomsky, 1999). It seems reasonable to assume that this is one of the reasons for the low turnouts in democratic elections, including in the United States (Ferguson & Rogers, 1981; Gilens, 2010). In Europe, much democratic policymaking has been shifted to the bureaucrats in Brussels. There is much to suggest that this democratic deficit will lead to democratic problems for the EU, and Brexit may be an early sign of such problems. The other sign of a lack of understanding of democratic processes was what happened in Greece in 2015. The people of Greece, opposing austerity measures, had voted in a democratic election for a new government. However, the 'Iron Triangle,' consisting of bureaucrats in Brussels, the European Central Bank, and the International Monetary Fund (IMF) wanted otherwise, with the consequence of profit being prioritized over people (Varoufakis, 2015).

The Great Illusion

In the new world order, private interests are taking over more and more power from democratic institutions (Chomsky, 2016a). This trend started in the 1980s, when neoliberalism became a dominant force in US policymaking and was characterized by Ronald Reagan's "trickle-down economics." The Norwegian proverb "When it rains on the priest, the sexton also gets wet" may be said to illustrate this trickle-down economics. In plain English, the idea is that if the wealthy are allowed to become wealthier, we will all benefit. We saw the same trend in Great Britain under Margaret Thatcher. Her government waged war on the trade unions. She set the market forces free and privatized everything that could be privatized.

The extreme centre, which includes the social democrats, supports this thinking. Free trade agreements were supposed to make everyone rich; for instance, consider the EU's efforts in 2016 to make free trade agreements with Canada (the Comprehensive Economic and Trade Agreement, or CETA) and the United States (the Transatlantic Trade and Investment Partnership, or TTIP).

The Great Illusion is as follows: economists believe that tax cuts at the top lead to increased value creation, and thus more to distribute to ordinary people. The truth is rather that economic growth could be even greater if other actions were taken: for instance, if the government adopted a policy of investing in infrastructure, information structure (info-structure), education, health, and so forth (Azmat, 2012; Varoufakis, 2015). In reality, the truth is that inequality accelerates when the wealthiest acquire even more money to spend (McGill, 2016; Piketty, 2016). The truth is that more consumption by the rich results in an increased demand for luxury goods, so that production veers away from meeting people's basic needs such as housing and work (Piketty, 2014; Stiglitz, 2013, 2016). The truth is that neoliberal ideology in its consequences is best for the extremely rich because they become even richer and their wealth is protected. The truth is that the unions are scattered like sawdust in feudal capitalism rather than being the proud oak tree they once were.

The plutocracy

In 2009, the richest 20% in the United States controlled about 84% of the wealth (Ariely, 2009). Developments suggest that the way capitalism works has changed. Inequality reinforces itself, and the 1% that is extremely rich is emerging as a separate class. We term this class here the 1% class.

The 1% class is elevated above the rest of the population. They live in their own newly constructed nation: the 'Mammon Nation.' In this nation they pay no taxes and only contribute charity to other nations. This charity is also used as part of the argument to explain why we all profit from some few being super-rich.

Even during the financial crisis,[1] between 2008 and 2010 the income of the 1% class in the United States increased by 11.6%, while the average income increase of the rest of the population was a mere 0.2% (Saez, 2012).[2] The same development occurred in most other countries, including developing countries such as India and China (Gaskarth, 2015; Swider, 2015).

This rich man's empire, that is the plutocracy or 1% class, has quietly and inconspicuously taken over the management of global capitalism, and thus also the economic development of various countries.

The three elements – Balkanization, the Great Illusion, and the plutocracy – are referred to here as feudal structures. In the following, we will describe, analyze, and discuss these elements individually and in interaction with each other.

The main question being investigated here is:

WHAT STRUCTURES AND PROCESSES ARE PROMOTING AND BOOSTING FEUDAL CAPITALISM?

The following three sub-questions are derived from the main question:

1   How does the Balkanization of democracy affect the development of feudal capitalism?

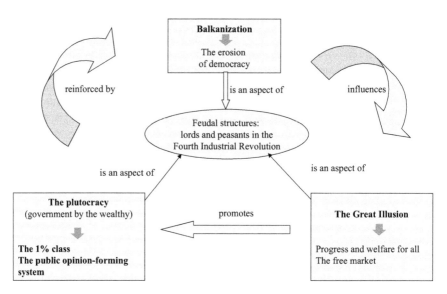

Figure 1.1 Feudal structures: lords and peasants in the Fourth Industrial Revolution

2   How does the Great Illusion affect the development of feudal capitalism?
3   How does the plutocracy affect the development of feudal capitalism?

We have visualized the introduction in Figure 1.1, which also shows how the rest of the chapter is organized.

Balkanization

The fear of democracy and fear of ordinary people's involvement in policymaking decisions are nothing new. In its early stages, democracy had its opponents; in the writings of Plato, Socrates is accredited with being critical of democracy as he reasoned that it could lead to freedom, and freedom would lead to complete chaos and the tyranny of the masses. People who are afraid of public opinion, direct democracy, and ordinary people having a voice in policy decisions thus have effective intellectual ballast in Socrates' views regarding democracy.

Balkanization here refers to profits being put before people's welfare and that a new world order is emerging.

Profits before people's welfare

When the workers at a slaughterhouse lose their jobs because of outsourcing, it is not necessarily because the business was unprofitable. It was just more profitable to move production to somewhere where costs are lower, such as Poland. In such cases, profit is put before people's welfare. When the workers at a wind turbine plant become sick because of epoxy poisoning, yet the plant management continue to use epoxy in construction, it tells us something about what matters most to the business. Thousands of similar cases describe the same: profit is considered to be more important than people's welfare.

The complexity at the beginning of the Fourth Industrial Revolution is so great and the public opinion industry so coherent and coordinated that people neither have the time nor the resources to see and understand what is in the process of happening. They become apathetic consumers who do not know what is going on or are unable to oppose developments (Chomsky, 2016: 2). This behaviour may be directly linked to the lack of democratic participation in elections and grassroots movements (Chomsky, 2016: 2).

If you were to single out one country that since the end of World War II has put profit over people, then the United States stands out. They have mainly set the terms for global discourse (Chomsky, 2016: 1), and among the G7 countries they have been a leading voice in global institutions such as the International Monetary Fund (IMF), the World Trade Organization (WTO), the International Bank for Reconstruction and Development (IBRD), and others.[3]

It is a generally held belief that in democratic states it is the people who most influence policy decisions. However, much American research (Bartels, 2008) has shown that it is the economic, cultural, and political elites that dominate and who have the greatest influence on policy decisions. In addition, those with low income have almost no influence on policy decision-making (Gilens, 2010). It is rather the interests of the economic, cultural, political, and intellectual elites that set the political agenda, and which are taken into account in policy decision-making.

As early as 1776, Adam Smith pointed out that if investors invested their capital in foreign countries they would profit from it, but to the detriment of the English population (Chomsky, 2016: 49). The leading economist of the period, David Ricardo, was also aware of this, but he hoped that the English capitalists would be satisfied with lower profits from domestic investment, thus creating prosperity in England (Chomsky, 2014: 150). Global capitalism works exactly as Smith and Ricardo foresaw it: it facilitates a free flow of capital, but profits are not lowered to improve domestic economies. This type of capitalism has given rise to the new global super-rich (Freeland, 2013), while some countries struggle to improve their domestic economies (Varoufakis, 2015).

The fact that profit is deemed more important than people's welfare does not cause the rich to feel the need to abolish democracy. They are smarter than that. Democracy has been transformed into a type of top-down bureaucracy, and it is argued that in a complicated world we need experts to govern. In other words, the economic and political elite govern through structures that may resemble democratic ones, but they are in reality more like feudal structures (Chomsky, 2012: 136–139). In addition to this, the public opinion industry convinces people that in a complex world, this is the best form of governance.

When it is necessary to have large capital resources to participate in politics, either in elections or to influence policy decisions, then the prerequisites for real democracy are absent because money takes precedence over people's needs and interests. Thomas Ferguson (1995) suggests that if you want to know who has the power in a political system then you should "follow the gold." If capital invests in political decision-making processes, then it is with good reason – the reason being the desire to profit from investments. This is a simple understanding of Ferguson's investment theory in the political system. What appears to have happened at the start of the Fourth Industrial Revolution is that capital and the extreme political centre have formed a golden alliance. In this alliance, profit is more important than people's welfare. In the staging of this alliance, the public opinion industry has convinced people that this is best for everyone. This is the origin of the Great Illusion.

Power lies largely in the abstract, or more specifically in taking control of abstraction. For instance, the word 'freedom' is an abstraction – that is, an abstract idea. The opposite of freedom may be said to be totalitarian structures, where lack of freedom is central. If you take over the power of abstraction – taking over the distinction between freedom and totalitarian structures – you have won every debate where the topic is social development, because everyone wants freedom but only the very few want totalitarian structures. However, if you want to introduce feudal structures that are totalitarian in their consequences, you do so by emphasizing that it is actually freedom and democracy that you wish to secure for the future. The one that takes over the power of abstraction takes advantage of the *gulag trap*[4] by setting up the distinction between freedom and totalitarian structures. If you go for freedom, you are in the territory of the liberals and will have lost the fight. If you go for totalitarian structures, you have also lost because you will be placed together with fascist or communist totalitarians. Of course, the strategy is not to be lured into this gulag trap. In other words, the best strategy is not to accept the distinction between freedom and totalitarian structures. Once you have accepted the distinction, you are caught in the gulag trap.

A new world order

One of the lessons learnt from the financial crisis triggered in autumn 2007, and which exploded in 2008, is that you cannot borrow your way out of a debt crisis (Coggan, 2011: 256–268). This is one of the reasons why it will take a long time before the consequences of the financial and social crisis will be eradicated. As long as the dollar is used by all countries as a reserve currency, the United States can print dollars without inflation being affected that much because the time lag between printing dollars and price rises is so great. On the other hand, the situation would totally change if the dollar were replaced by a pool of reserve currencies such as the euro, renminbi,[5] and yen. Whatever the developments concerning the world's reserve currency, China will become a serious competitor of the American economic, political, and military hegemony, especially in Asia. However, China owns so much of the American debt that the two countries are tied together by a mutual economic bond.

Internationalization may be understood as an interaction between nations. Globalization may be understood as an interaction 'over and beyond nations' (Monbiot, 2004: 22). Globalization may be expressed by the following points:

1   Removal of control of capital flows
2   Removal of trade barriers
3   The increased influence of the major global businesses
4   Increased economic inequality
5   Increased productivity through new technology.

Productivity growth is not always the result of technological innovation. Chomsky points out that the use of the whip and the gun in the early cotton industry resulted in a large increase in productivity (2015: X). Robotized production has major consequences for most people. Some are positive, but many are very negative, for instance job losses, the wages of non-automated jobs being forced downwards by competition, and the emergence of the 'working poor' (Shipler, 2005). The working poor are those who have difficulty in supporting themselves and their families, despite the fact they might both have two jobs. The emergence of the precariat (Standing, 2014a, 2016) is also one of the consequences of globalization and robotization. The precariat is described and analyzed in more detail in Chapter 3. In brief, we can say that the precariat is a new class of workers who are not permanently employed but are hired on contract; the contracts are often of short duration and poorly paid. The precariat consists of people who have both lower and higher education, immigrants, foreigners, and people who are opposed to the elite.

The new world order is still based on the United States as the leading superpower. The growing economic inequality is based on an economic ideology advocated by the public opinion–forming system in the West. "Everything has been globalised except our consent," says Monbiot (2004: 1).

Almost without exception, the elite say they use democratic principles of freedom as the governing basis of global capitalism (Monbiot, 2004: 1). Used in this way, the concept of freedom has no meaning.

The largest development that will shape the new order is major technology companies such as Google and Facebook. They have the possibility of transforming democracy into a sham-democracy. If they wish to, these companies can manipulate people's perceptions and opinions so that the outcome of so-called democratic elections is determined by what best serves the owners of the major technology companies. This can be done by altering algorithms and parameters in their search engines (Barrat, 2015; Case, 2016; Hanson, 2016). In addition to the fact that large technological companies have the built-in ability to control the shaping of people's opinions, most people are usually obedient and loyal to the superstructures they have been socialized into. Consequently, they can be even more easily controlled according to the wishes of the elite.

Globalization has laid the foundation for the new world order. Technology development supports global profits. The World Bank and the IMF as well as various trade agreements reinforce developments where profit is placed above people's welfare, which we witnessed in the case of Greece, as mentioned above (Varoufakis, 2015). We can also see it clearly in the fact that more than 100 million children are denied a basic education (OECD, 2002).

The most serious aspect of the emergence of the new world order is that power has migrated away from democratic control to power centres that most people don't even know exist. Neither do most people know how this power is exercised, what is done, or the consequences of decisions made. The decisions made have a very great impact on people's lives. One of the consequences that is easiest to understand is that wage earners around the globe compete with each other, forcing down real wages (Hines, 2000). The fall in wages further increases the profits of capital owners, which further increases economic inequalities (Standing, 2014, 2014a). This is the 'freedom' the rich talk about – the freedom of wage earners to compete for below-poverty wage jobs.

Another consequence of this development is that individual states lose control of their own economy (Wilkinson & Pickett, 2009) because the global economy is governed by large capital funds, major international corporations, and the institutions that support them.

Colin Hines proposes that a strategy to counter this trend would be to introduce positive discrimination nationally and locally (2000). This can be done by imposing taxes on financial transactions, using protective tariffs and other protectionist interventions. Hines also believes that the control of national industry and services should be in the hands of individual national states. It is the local as opposed to the global Hines views as a solution to the negative effects of globalization. Hines also suggests adopting common standards for working conditions so that one country cannot compete with another country based on the fact that workers sell their labour at a continually lower level to survive.

Regardless of one's views regarding trade, history has shown that trade has promoted value creation since Roman times. We have also seen that the embargoes placed on Cuba, Iran, and Russia have had major negative economic consequences for these countries. Thus, the problem is not trade but how the profits of trade are distributed. Nor is the problem financial capital but who owns the capital and how the profits are distributed.

The description of Balkanization is visualized and summarized in Figure 1.2.

The Great Illusion

Anyone who expresses opinions that could be financially detrimental to the dominant elite is viewed in a suspicious light by the public opinion–forming system, which is also owned by the elite (McChesney, 2016: 8). The free market is considered to be the only rational ideology and hence the only sensible way to organize production, distribution, and consumption. The mantra of the 'free' market chanted by its advocates claims that maintenance of the free market is a service carried out by the rich for the benefit of the poor to make the poor richer (McChesney, 2016: 8).

However, the real truth is something else. In all areas where neoliberalism has prevailed there has been "a massive increase in social and economic inequality" (McChesney, 2016: 8). The only argument it seems that is advanced by the neoliberalists is not based on empirical research but on an ideological slogan from the

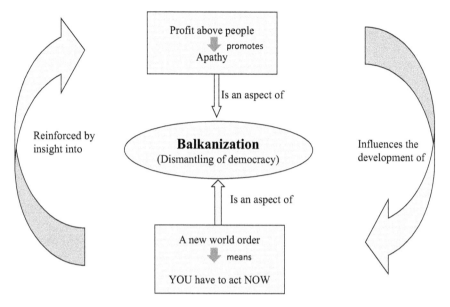

Figure 1.2 The Balkanization of democracy

Thatcher era: TINA (i.e. 'There is no alternative'). This, of course, is not the case. There are always alternatives (TAAA).

The advocates of neoliberalism and the so-called free market state that without neoliberalism and the free market there can be no democratic free society. The truth is rather that neoliberalism represents the ugly face of capitalism, a face its proponents proudly wear. Without shame, they refer to neoliberalist ideologues such as Ayn Rand, whose fictional works may be summed up in one sentence: what is good for me is good for everybody. Interestingly, this also reflects Adam Smith's ideology. Bourgeois economics from the 1700s up until today form an economic system based on selfishness. 'Freedom' is used as a cloak for this selfishness. This is evident in the writings of Milton Friedman, a strong advocate of neoliberal economics (Friedman, 2002).

Profit is the driving force of capitalism. The free market is held as a kind of religious belief by the neoliberalists; thus, anyone who proposes that people's welfare should go before profit is considered 'anti-democratic' and viewed with suspicion as if they were totalitarian communists. This illusion is propagated by the opinion–forming system of feudal capitalism through fictional works, such as the novels of Ayn Rand; through economic theories, such as those of the Nobel Prize–winner Milton Friedman; and through the ideas of neoliberal politicians, such as Reagan and Thatcher. Neoliberal democracy sets the free market as the highest of its democratic institutions. Those who argue against the free market and neoliberalism are pigeonholed together with the likes of Stalin and Pol Pot.

However, neoliberal democracy has resulted in capitalism acquiring feudal structures, which we now see the contours of in feudal capitalism. Another consequence of the neoliberal ideology, where profit is put before ordinary people's needs, is a creeping political apathy. This is evident in the poor election turnouts. For instance, in the United States only 33% voted in the congressional elections of 1998, and only 47% voted in the Russian State Duma election of 2016. A sentiment held by many is this: what is the point of voting when the decisions that affect ordinary people's lives are decided by the neoliberal market? Thus, people vote with their feet and show that they do not care as long as political elections have little or no influence on their lives.

Most people believe in the mythology of the free market. Governments and the opinion–forming system make sure that the myth is maintained. Despite the fact that the myth has competition as a prerequisite, there is extreme regulation of competition due to the globalization of businesses and the merger processes that are a consequence of globalization (McChesney, 2016: 13).

Globalization is not a law of nature. Its development has been facilitated for political reasons. The United States has taken the lead in promoting globalization policies. The social mechanisms used are trade agreements. The consequence is that the rich have become richer. The myth that is spread is that everyone profits from globalization. However, empirical data tells us another story:[6]

1   An IMF report from 2016 states that 20% of the children in the United States live in poverty.
2   The same report states that 14% of the US population lives in poverty.
3   Thirty-three per cent of the children of single mothers in the United States live in poverty.
4   Only 40% of the poor are employed.
5   Further, the IMF report provides the alarming information that more unequal income distribution has weakened growth in output, income, and jobs.

Other data that contradicts the official myth include the following: Italy has had little real growth in wages in the last 25 years. Unemployment among young people is 39%. The general unemployment rate is more than 11%. The economy has fallen by more than 8% since 2008.[7]

It has been necessary to maintain the myth and illusion that globalization and the free market is something everyone profits from (Chomsky, 2016). Thus, the Great Illusion has been maintained despite the fact that prosperity has been reduced for ordinary people but has increased strongly for the rich. British workers are worse off today than 20 years ago, and between 2007 and 2015 real wages fell by 10%. Between 65% and 70% of households in the United States and Europe have had a drop in real wages during the period 2005–2014.[8]

The Great Illusion has functioned as a bulwark against what could have been. When illusion lies like a fog over people's consciousness, the prevailing conditions are accepted as if they are a law of nature. However, there is no law of nature in this context. The current global economic conditions are the consequence of willed political actions – the result of policy decisions that have led to the desired economic outcomes.

It should not be forgotten that the development and maintenance of this illusion is carried out by journalists, academics, politicians, teachers, nurses, bureaucrats, military systems, technocratic systems, and so on. These people have with commitment and conviction disseminated this message. They are committed to conveying this illusion, which of course is not perceived as an illusion by them. They are like Raskin (2015: 11–12) says, testifying to an idea that they believe in. It is a pity that so many families must bear the consequences of this ideology.

The plutocracy

It should be made clear that the 1% class became super-rich because of political decisions that were made. It was no economic law of nature that created the oligarchs in Russia or the 1% class in the rest of the world. The plutocracy resulted from a willed political action carried out by those with the political power to make the decisions that resulted in this development.

A strong relationship between the 1% class and the elite in the political system has been developed. In this way, the economic decision-making system and the political decision-making system are linked. The elites of these two systems reinforce each other and strengthen their respective economic and political muscles. This also promotes the emergence of a new governing system: the plutocracy. This governance system consists of the economic, political, cultural, and intellectual elite. This elite governs and controls developments in the Fourth Industrial Revolution. Of interest in this context is the fact that the 1% class invests in the public opinion–forming system, such as newspapers, television, and social media, and these consciously steer, control, and shape public opinion.

Adam Smith was aware of the possible development towards a plutocracy. As early as 1776 he wrote:

> All for ourselves, and nothing for other people, seems in every age of the world to have been the vile maxim of the masters of mankind. As soon, therefore, as they could find a method of consuming the whole value of their rents themselves, they had no dispositions to share them with any other person.
>
> (Adam Smith, 1976: 418)

We must emphasize here that this is no quote from Karl Marx, but Adam Smith, the founder of the classic bourgeois economic ideology.

In the following, we describe, analyze, and discuss the plutocracy. First, we will discuss the 1% class, and then the public opinion–forming system.

The 1% class

The Nobel Prize winners in economics, Stiglitz (2013) and Shiller,[9] both say that the main problem we face in today's economic system is increasing inequality.

The increasing difference in wage income and capital income may be regarded as one of the largest threats to social structures (Dorling, 2015: 1). The greed of the top 1% class is described by the public opinion–forming system as a prerequisite for everyone having it better. This Great Illusion is socially designed so effectively that many believe in this Goebbelsian fact.[10]

It is of advantage here to make a distinction in the 1% class between the super-rich and the mega-rich. The super-rich in England have been defined as those who have an annual income of over £160,000 before tax (Gribb et al., 2013). The mega-rich are those who have an income far above this amount. It is essentially the mega-rich that dominate and control the public opinion–forming system.

Sam Wilkin (2016) has studied how people have become super-rich. He has investigated the super-rich in the Roman Empire, the money barons in the late 1800s and the 1900s (Morgan, Carnegie, Rockefeller, Gould, Vanderbilt), and others. His investigation also includes the Russian oligarchs, Indian billionaires, the Chinese super-rich, the information technology (IT) world's super-rich, US billionaires, Mexican financial leaders, and others. The study has led to a theory of how to become super-rich. Wilkin's theory[11] (2016: 327–371) may be summarized by the following ten statements:

1 Don't be the best, but be the only one who supplies the product or service.
2 Don't seek out competition, but establish yourself where no competition exists.
3 If someone enters the market at a later point, eliminate the competition by acquisitions.
4 Become big. Size means something; being small makes you vulnerable.
5 Be brutal in business: that is, good ethics are only for the simple-minded.
6 Build alliances and networks focusing on the economic, political, social, and cultural systems.
7 Take advantage of the relationships you've built up over time.
8 You have to own the business. Being an employee will never make you rich.
9 Connect closely to financial sources (i.e. banks or other institutions). You must always have access to capital.
10 Connect very closely to the political power elite so that laws are made to the advantage of your business. You keep to the laws, but it's easy when they are made for you.

This shows that the strategy most of the super-rich have used is not for people with weak nerves, high morals, or a great capacity for empathy. In Wilkin's foreword, he writes: "You guessed it, the game is rigged" (Wilkin, 2016: vi). In the literature on the success of individuals and businesses, the importance of hard work and competitiveness is often stressed. However, according to Wilkin, the opposite is the case. The survival and success of systems is largely arranged. Those who enter the competition on equal terms are largely outcompeted, bought up, or bankrupted. The 1% class has managed to arrange the game to their own advantage. They only do what is in their interests, even when they donate to charity.

The 1% class do not do anything illegal. They are only following the advice of Adam Smith and all the classical economists who followed in his footsteps: if everyone does what is best for themselves, this will also be best for society (Smith, 1976: 410–418). However, this is of course an ideological statement, not an economic fact. There is no evidence that supports this statement, no matter how many times it is claimed to be the truth. The consequences of following the precept of this statement have been increasing inequality (Stiglitz, 2013, 2016).

The difference between the rich and wage earners has increased (Piketty, 2014, 2016) – a development that is a classical recipe for social rebellion (Bauman, 2013). This rebellion may take on many forms. The populist political right wing has channelled the rebellion against various types of elites. In Greece and Spain, the political left wing has channelled the rebellion against profits and capital. In the British Labour Party, the rebellion has led to the left-wing candidate Jeremy Corbyn being elected twice as leader of the party, despite the fact that the elite of the British Labour Party opposed Corbyn and proposed their own candidate. In the United States, Donald Trump won the Republican nomination and became president in 2016. In the Democratic Party, Bernie Sanders won the political left side in opposition to Hillary Clinton. The social uprising takes on different forms and is expressed as both right and left-wing revolts in the political landscape. What seems to be a common denominator of this social rebellion is that people are "sick and tired of the establishment" (Wilkin, 2016: vii).

The underlying cause of the rebellion may be related to the lobbying activities of the 1% aimed at the political elite, which has resulted in laws being passed that defend their interests but which has also led to hundreds of thousands of jobs being exported to low-cost countries. The question the individual worker should ask is: if one million foreign workers can do your job at a lower salary, why should you have the job? Millions of jobs have been transferred from industrial areas to developing countries. Among other things, this has resulted in many people losing their livelihoods while making the super-rich even richer. Consequently, there has been an angry reaction directed towards the economic, social, political, cultural, and intellectual elites.

The argument claiming that development of globalism and the free market is natural and necessary is part of the Great Illusion. The Great Illusion is that everyone benefits from globalization, free trade agreements, and inequality. However, the negative effects of this global development are felt by the majority of workers in the United Kingdom, the United States, Greece, Spain, and other countries. The rich get richer and the workers and middle classes suffer (Freeland, 2013: 4). The wage earners in the global economy compete against each other resulting in them having to accept lower wages if they are to have work, which results in greater profits for the capital owners. Thus profit has become a right, not an opportunity. If profits are threatened by environmental legislation, higher minimum wages, taxes on harmful products, and so on, capital is simply moved to regions of the world that have more 'friendly' conditions.

The 1% class are acquiring a new identity now that they are getting richer and richer while increasing their influence over policy decision-making. This identity is supra-national and can be viewed as deriving from their global thinking.

Increasingly, they are becoming a separate 'nation,' which Freeland (2013: 5) calls "the nation of mammon." In this nation, profit has become a right for the rich, a right that will make them even richer. To facilitate this, the wages share of profits must be reduced.

In this new nation, the tax rate is zero. The 1% class takes advantage of the workforce in the 'local' nations, so that employees compete with each other to lower wages, thus increasing the profits of the 1% class. The super-rich are fully aware of the division of the global economy between the 1% class and the other 99%; however, the latter are largely unaware of this development. The reason is quite simple: they are caught up in the Great Illusion that is spread by the public opinion–forming system.

Thus the emerging nation is made up only of the 1% class. They exploit the local 'nations' while living in their 'mammon nation,' disconnected from the 99% others. Most of us never see them because they live separately. They have their own private aircraft. They socialize with others in the 1% class and live in a manner similar to the English upper classes of the 1700s and 1800s.

The 1% class exploit the theory and ideology of the free market to maintain their wealth and power. However, the plutocracy makes use of a system which is quite different from the theory and ideology they seemingly argue for. Although they argue for 'free' competition and a 'free' market, they do all they can to prevent competition that can harm their profits. They maintain in trade agreements that profit is a right they are entitled to protect when legitimate democratic assemblies attempt to make restrictions reducing their profits.[12] It's not just that profit is put above people's welfare: profit becomes a right that reduces democratic control.

As more and more people gain insight into the luxurious lifestyle of the 1% class, more people will realize that we can no longer afford to subsidize the rich. This applies, inter alia, to lower taxes on interest income than on wage income, the subsidization they receive on housing due to deduction schemes, favourable tax rules, and so on. This type of subsidization is given to encourage a particular form of behaviour. The richest man in 2001, Warren Buffett, expressed this quite precisely: "Actually, there's been class warfare going on for the last 20 years, and my class has won. We're the ones that have gotten our tax rates reduced."[13]

If we ignore the 1% class and investigate the remaining 99%, we see an interesting development, at least in the United Kingdom. While there is increasing inequality between the 1% class and the others, there is growing income similarity in the remaining 99% (Dorling, 2015: 3). On the one hand inequality is increasing, but on the other there is greater equality within the 99% (Gribb et al., 2013: 30–45). This is something one should be aware of concerning the argument which claims that the vast majority of the population are experiencing greater equality, as measured by the Gini coefficient (Gribb et al., 2013: 40). This is a correct statement, but nevertheless incorrect. The error lies *not* in considering the difference between the 1% and 99% others, but *only* the development within the 99% (Dorling, 2013: 1, 2015: 3–5).

The average income for a family with no children in the United Kingdom in 2012 was about £23,000 per year. The 10% with the lowest income have approximately £11,000 per year, mainly from welfare payments (Dorling, 2015: 5).

An interesting historical observation is that before World War I there was increasing inequality. The same trend could be found before the Great Depression in the 1930s. Today, we are seeing some of the same developments, where countries such as the United States, Canada, and the United Kingdom are leading in the competition for having the greatest inequality between the 1% and the 99% others (Dorling, 2015: 15). It is often said in the debate about income equalization that it would have no effect if you took from the super-rich and mega-rich and distributed it to the other 99%. This is incorrect. To take the United Kingdom as an example:

> In the UK today, the poorest couple could double their annual income and the median households could be 10 per cent better off if the richest 1 per cent took just five times the average income, rather than fifteen times.
>
> (Dorling, 2015: 19–20)

Concerns about the negative affect the increasing inequality and greed of the 1% class can have on the capitalist system have also reached the defenders of this system (Stiglitz, 2013, 2016; Krugman, 2017). Thus, it is no longer only the political left that attacks the greed of the 1% class and the negative consequences of the enormous inequality of the global economy. They also have alliance partners with those who defend the capitalist system. It is unlikely that the 1% class consists of more 'evil' people than the rest of the population; it is only the consequences of enormous inequality that lead to sorrow, pain, lost dreams, hunger, and the broken expectations of millions of people. In Britain alone there were 3.5 million children living in poverty in 2012 (Dorling, 2015: 238 note 16). Between 2010 and 2015, the standard of living in Britain fell for the whole population except the 1% class (Dorling, 2015: 189).

"Those who are not so well off economically are just envious of the rich" is the argument used by the rich and their intellectual mercenaries. Yes, of course they are envious. When they see their buying power being reduced and their children living in poverty, and when they have to stand in line to get an underpaid job, why shouldn't they be envious? The poor are not exactly Jesuit monks who have sold everything they own for their faith. On the contrary, they hardly own anything and have every reason to be envious. They have every reason to be angry when they see their children living an unworthy and pitiful life without the opportunity of fulfilling the dream of a better life.

The point here is, however, that the public opinion–forming system, that is the intellectual mercenaries, has portrayed envy as a Christian sin. In the Catholic faith, envy is defined as one of the seven deadly sins. The intellectual mercenaries do this for good reason – to safeguard the wealth of their masters. Then come the cherries on the rhetorical cake of the intellectual mercenaries, the clichés one often hears:

> We must teach the poor to budget better.
>
>   The poor must learn to look after the pennies so the pounds will take care of themselves.

We're all in the same boat.
Hard work leads to prosperity.
We should all be friends.
Be grateful for the charity that the rich give to the needy.

The 1% class sincerely believe that their wealth is a prerequisite for making every-one's life better. This thinking may be likened to the lion that claims while sinking his teeth into a zebra that he's only doing it to help the remaining zebras because there will be more grazing for those left. The intellectual mercenaries argue in this manner to protect the wealth of the 1% class. Of course, one can argue in this way, but it is simply a case of pea-brained logic, to put it bluntly, and the development of a Goebbelsian fact.

The public opinion–forming system

The 1% class, directly or through funds they control, buy up media such as news-papers, TV channels, and various social media to control the shaping of people's opinions. Through social construction, they control the development of public opinion about 'the facts.' This social construction of facts is similar to the con-struction of Goebbelsian facts. A Goebbelsian fact is based on the idea that if a lie is big enough and repeated often enough, it will be believed. To achieve this, the 1% class pays leading intellectuals who produce these Goebbelsian facts. These intellectual mercenaries construct arguments about the necessity and the useful-ness of economic inequality in society. They carry out their activities using vari-ous platforms, often including think tanks.

In Figure 1.3 we have visualized aspects of the opinion-forming system. When we say aspects, this is because there are many other aspects that we could inves-tigate but we have chosen to examine the three that are visualized in Figure 1.3.

Figure 1.3 shows also how we explain and discuss the public opinion–forming system.

Media control

Media control has a huge impact on how people think, what they talk about, what they are interested in, what they are indifferent to, and how their political attitudes are shaped and changed (Chomsky, 2002: 9–13). The plutocracy, which controls the media, also largely controls our perception of what constitutes democracy and democratic processes. The classic perception of democracy found in any ency-clopaedia is as follows: people should be able to participate in the relationships that concern their lives, and the information and resources they need to do this are freely available.

However, the prevailing practice is different. In most countries, people do not have the opportunity to participate in the government of their country, directly or indirectly. The information they would need to do this is largely not accessible (Chomsky, 2002: 10). This was exemplified by the veil of secrecy surrounding

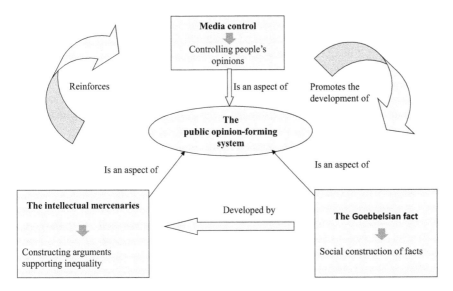

Figure 1.3 The public opinion–forming system

the negotiations for the Comprehensive and Economic Trade Agreement (CERT) between the EU and Canada. Absolutely no EU citizens were given access to the negotiating process. If any elected representatives wished to scrutinize the draft agreement, they had to leave behind any cameras, phones, pens and paper and so forth. Everything had to be kept secret from the public.

The media and power

Since the end of World War II, the United States has installed and supported various military juntas around the globe – in Central and South America, Africa, Europe, and Asia. In the respective countries, these military juntas have carried out torture and mass murder of their own populations.[14] The media has largely suppressed or 'forgotten' to report what was happening in these countries. In the case of Latin America, the American media has argued that the terror of the juntas was necessary and the result of having to combat left-wing guerrilla movements (Chomsky, 2015: 12–13). In other contexts, it is argued that although the terror inflicted is monstrous, it is necessary to prevent even worse terror that a communist regime would supposedly have used (Chomsky, 2015: 13–16).

With one exception,[15] says Chomsky (2015a: 17), the United States has never overthrown, de-stabilized, or invaded countries run by right-wing military junta regimes. It is in democratically elected leftist governments where the United States has intervened, such as Chile (1973), Guatemala (1954), Iran (1953), and Brazil (1964), and the left-wing revolutions in Cuba (1959) and in Vietnam (1954–1973). The military junta model seems to have worked well for the United

States. The CIA and the Sixth Fleet have operated in unison, such as when they supported the 1964 Brazilian coup d'état that led to the overthrow of President Goulart by the military junta. Torture and death squads are the instruments that have been used to sweep the path clear for capital investment.

Media techniques

There are various media techniques that are used to influence people's opinions:

1　The first technique is silence. You only report to a small extent what happened or is happening.
2　A second media technique is to downplay the events or explain them as 'necessary,' for instance to prevent the establishment of a communist government in the United States' backyard.
3　A third media technique is an imbalanced focus. For instance, Western media focuses disproportionality on human rights abuses in the Soviet Union and Cuba, while curiously remaining largely silent about similar human rights abuses carried out by the Chinese communist government against the Chinese population (which has been documented several times). The reason that springs to mind is that China is positive towards the free flow of capital.
4　A fourth media technique is to pick out some facts and focus on them while downplaying or ignoring other facts in order to steer people's attention in a particular direction.
5　A fifth media technique is to construct lies and create myths to manipulate public opinion. To influence public opinion for the US support of Kuwait in the First Gulf War, it was widely published that Iraqi soldiers were murdering newly born Kuwaiti infants. The story ran as follows: a 15-year-old Kuwaiti girl, Nayirah, in a tearful testimony broadcast on American TV, told how she had seen with her own eyes Iraqi soldiers commit terrible atrocities in the maternity ward in Kuwait where she worked as a volunteer. The Iraqi soldiers, she said, had stormed the ward, taken the babies out of the incubators, and thrown them on the ground, leaving them to die. This emotional testimony outraged the American public. However, it was later shown that the whole story was just one big lie. It was proven that the girl was staying in the United States during the time she claimed to have been in Kuwait. A big lie was also spread in the build-up to the second invasion of Iraq (the Second Gulf War) with the aim of mustering up international support. US Secretary of State Colin Powell presented a case to the United Nations which he knew to be false, or at best doubtful. It was reported that the United States had secured intelligence that Saddam Hussein possessed weapons of mass destruction. However, the UN's independent inquiry to investigate the allegations, led by the Swede Hans Blix,[16] found no evidence of a nuclear weapons programme in Iraq. However, the American lie was nevertheless effective. An alliance of willing states was created to aid the United States in their

invasion of Iraq.[17] Today, we know the consequences all too well: Iraq has descended into inner chaos and ISIS has gained considerable control in Iraq, Syria, and other regions.

6 A sixth media technique is to close down newspapers and other public opinion–forming media. For instance, on 10 October 2016, an owner consortium in Hungary, Mediaworks, with immediate effect closed down the largest opposition newspaper, *Népszabadság*. On the previous Friday (7 October), the newspaper had reported on its front page a case of corruption against the political leadership of Hungary.[18] This example demonstrates clearly in this case how the free word is only free as long as it serves the interests of power.

7 A seventh Western media technique is to downplay the West's violations by comparing communist violations with something worse than those committed by the Nazis during World War II.[19] In this manner, the idea is established that socialists and Nazis use the same methods, although they have different goals. The idea is spread through several channels, including the *Reader's Digest* (which has tens of millions of readers), *TV Guide*, *New York Review of Books*, *New Republic*, and so on (Chomsky, 2015a: 21).

8 An eighth media technique is a systematic under-prioritization of historical events that one does not wish to figure prominently in people's consciousness. For instance, this applies to the United States and the West's intervention and removal of democratically elected leaders, such as in Chile and Iran.

9 A ninth media technique is what may be termed self-censorship. Journalists do not write about news topics they feel would be in conflict with the owners' interests. Nor do they write about that which might challenge the dominant logic of society. They select news topics that are considered suitable and de-select those that are considered unsuitable. In the present day, journalists are afraid to lose their jobs as there are few vacant ones.

10 A tenth media technique is the various combinations of the nine others. In this way, we arrive at $(n(n-1))$, that is about 72 different types of media techniques that may be utilized to control people's thoughts.

Goebbelsian facts

Propaganda as a concept was created in 1622 when Pope Gregory XV, fearing the spread of Protestantism, established an office for propaganda for the Catholic faith (Miller, 2005: 9). Later, the authorities began to use propaganda to promote their own interests. In the 1800s and 1900s, it became clear that public opinion was a force that had to be shaped, managed, and maintained (Miller, 2005: 12). Today, propaganda has changed in both form and content; the actual understanding of the term has changed as well. There is less talk about propaganda, which has a negative association, and more about 'public relations' (PR), communication, and influence. However, the purpose has only changed to a small extent. The purpose is to control public opinion. This is evident from Gustave Le Bon, who wrote about the phenomenon as early as 1895 in *The Crowd* (Le Bon, 2014).

Today, we call it propaganda when totalitarian states try to control public opinion. Yet we call it 'the search for truth' when the Western media, owned by funds or a few capital owners, attempts to influence and shape public opinion.

There are numerous examples of how propaganda has been used throughout history to influence people's thinking. During World War I, President Woodrow Wilson established the Creel Committee to turn an anti-war population into one that was willing and wanted to go to war against Germany (Chomsky, 2002: 11). Accounts of German atrocities were published in the United States by the British Ministry of Propaganda, such as the undocumented account that German soldiers killed Belgian babies by spitting them on their bayonets (Chomsky, 2002: 12). Of course, the British government propaganda had a clear intention behind spreading such stories: to control people's minds, thinking, and attitudes regarding the war. The British Ministry of Propaganda, in reporting these undocumented atrocities in the United States, contributed to convincing the American public to enter the war.

Just after World War I,[20] the Americans used the same methods to create fear and promote hatred of all types of socialism and communism.

Goebbels utilized such ideas before and during World War II (Longerich, 2015: 205–391). Something similar may be said to be happening today – the people in power wish to control people's thinking. When the public opinion–forming system influences people's thinking, they are treating people like Pavlov's[21] dogs. A chapter heading in Longerich's biography on Goebbels is titled "Taking Firm Control of the Inner Discipline of a People" (Longerich, 2015: 273). This expresses the main purpose of a Goebbelsian fact: to control the formation of public opinion.

Some call this propaganda, but the Western 'democratic' version terms this public information. However, whatever term is used, the purpose is the same: to influence people's opinions in a certain direction.

The opinion-forming system makes use of the fact that our understanding of the world is socially constructed. Consequently, people in positions of power (e.g. the government) feel it is necessary to actively participate in this social construction. Following the logic of this interpretation, journalists may almost be considered to be 'civil servants,' something which Goebbels clearly understood (Longerich, 2015: 278). However, viewing journalists in a free democratic society as an extended arm of those in power contradicts our idea of an independent fourth estate. Moreover, there is an ever-increasing tendency of progressive concentration of the media in a few large media houses. There is also a growing tendency that the survival of the various media depends on advertising revenue. Consequently, it may be said that Goebbelsian facts are developed in relation to the owner groups that pay for advertising space. What is common to those who own media and those who deliver content to the media is that both depend on money flowing in to the media houses. If this is a correct analysis, then it follows logically that those who deliver content to the media will largely be ruled by those who own these media.

Goebbels was fully aware of this type of control of opinion formation, and he focused on this by having a strong grip on cultural policy (Longerich, 2015: 281).

While Goebbels wanted to have unified news, the development in the Western world today seems to be geared towards controlling the media through ownership. In both contexts the aim is the same: to control public opinion.

Another aspect of Goebbelsian facts is the way groupthink works (Janis, 1982). Through groupthink, an assumption becomes the truth within the group which individuals in the group conform to: Janis (1982) showed how bad decisions made regarding the Bay of Pigs disaster (1961) were due to groupthink.

Owen Jones' book *The Establishment: And How They Get Away With It* (Jones, 2015) shows how Goebbelsian facts are spread today in the United Kingdom. Jones provides examples and shows with clarity how the ruling class (the establishment) in the United Kingdom promotes its own views, permeating these so they also become the views and opinions of the public. Consequently, these views become the dominant logic in society that most people relate to as if they were Pavlov's dogs. Jones' book answers the question: why do people think the way they do? He shows us how lies are turned into the truth, that is Goebbelsian facts. He also shows us how the British government, the establishment, and the opinion-forming system interact to create the public 'truth.' He shows how public opinion is created by the owners of the major corporations through various front-men and willing intellectual mercenaries, who control the formation of public opinion. The purpose of controlling public opinion is quite simple: "to consolidate the interests of the few at the expense of the many," writes Owen Jones of the *Huffington Post* (as quoted on the cover page of Jones' book).[22] Jones shows how the big businesses go about avoiding taxes and how lobbying is a necessary social mechanism to accomplish this.

The lobbyists for banks, the oil industry, and other important industries use lobbying to influence policy decisions. This is often called providing information to government decision-makers that is of interest to the company and the public in general. The reality is rather that those who pay for the lobbying only seek to gain advantages for their particular business. Therefore, they pay large sums to public relations agencies. Warren Buffett's words cited earlier are of interest in this context: "Actually, there's been class warfare going on for the last 20 years, and my class has won. We're the ones that have gotten our tax rates reduced."[23] Is there really anyone who thinks that Buffett and his class pay large sums to the PR agencies because of their love of informing the public?

The intellectual mercenaries

The leading intellectuals participate in various types of commissions, think tanks, and the media to shape people's opinions and create public consent for specific political policies.

The mindset of the intellectual mercenaries is that society is so complex that ordinary people are unable to understand it. Therefore, society must be led by a competent and selected class of responsible and intelligent people who govern society for the people. This is the intellectual elite, the intellectual mercenaries, who are strongly linked to the 1% class.[24]

In order to maintain their prosperity, the 1% class engages the leading intellectuals to find arguments to legitimize the uneven distribution of economic resources. The intellectual mercenaries who choose to serve the 1% class acquire power precisely through this execution of their activities. The thinking is simple: you attain power by providing services to those who have economic power. The intellectual mercenaries consist of economists, social scientists, political scientists, lawyers, military officers, the police, intelligence agencies, priests, bishops, and occasionally even a pope.[25] These people provide services, consciously, and in some cases unconsciously, in order to control and steer public opinion. In the United States, we have seen this in the case of the Creel Committee and through McCarthy's witch-hunt of 'Communists' – where everyone on the political left was defined as a potential traitor. We have seen how the desire to control public opinion has resulted in the policy of spreading lies prior to and during the First and Second Gulf Wars. Lies were used to manipulate people to support the First Gulf War, which involved among other things a ground assault of Kuwait; and the Second Gulf War, which involved the invasion of Iraq.

The intellectual mercenaries may be considered engineers of public opinion. Through various PR promotions they shape public opinion. The intellectual mercenaries carry out the intellectual assassination of people's opinions. This has been done whenever public opinion has been of importance to the people in power. The 1% class have won the class struggle with the help of the intellectual mercenaries.[26] The people who maintain the 1% class may be pictured as medieval knights who protect and wage war for their masters. The myths that these intellectual mercenaries create include:

1   The unemployed are lazy and only grab for themselves what others have to work for.
2   The unemployed must be motivated to work by taking away the little they have. This was the case in Denmark, when on 1 October 2016 state benefits were significantly reduced, the so-called cash aid ceiling which affected 33,000 Danes.[27]
3   The rich create the jobs.
4   The rich pay the most in taxes to the public treasury.
5   The rich use their money for charitable purposes.
6   Everyone has the opportunity to get rich: it's just a case of working hard and being target-oriented.

However, the intellectual mercenaries write little about what happens to those who are left out. There are of course exceptions, such as the report in the Danish newspaper *Politiken*, which describes what happens to the unemployed:

- Your self-esteem is eroded.
- You slowly but surely get the feeling of being invisible to others.
- You notice the rejection of people around you.
- You begin to question yourself and your abilities.

- Your family is broken up.
- You feel inferior and find that your close family and friends are ashamed of the position you've got yourself into.[28]

Conclusion

The main question that was investigated in this chapter is:

WHAT STRUCTURES AND PROCESSES ARE PROMOTING AND BOOSTING FEUDAL CAPITALISM?

We have answered this question by describing, analyzing, and discussing three topics:

1   Balkanization, where we investigated the dismantling of democracy.
2   The Great Illusion, where the argument is that what benefits the wealthy also benefits the poor. To achieve this situation, the focus is moved to the free market. The reality is that the free market is strongly controlled, and freedom in this market only exists in economics textbooks. Practical experience indicates the opposite.
3   The plutocracy, where we have shown how a wealthy elite are controlling not only the financial system, but also the political, judicial, cultural, and intellectual spheres.

Free competition and the free market don't make the wealthy rich. The 1% class has been created through the exercise of control over markets by means of laws that serve the interests of the elite. In theory, no one can become super-wealthy in a free and competitive market. The reason why some people become super-wealthy nonetheless is that they have worked in various ways to remove the competition while holding after-dinner speeches about the merits of competition. If one is to find out why some of the super-wealthy became so rich, one should try to find the smoking gun. In other words, what is it that they are hiding in their past which put them in a position to become so rich? In any event, the smoking gun will not be concealing any concerns about the morality of their actions. It is the secret that points to the 'tipping point' – the point at which their profits rose more than those of other people.

In every success that the 1% elite can claim, there are people and organizations – and sometimes whole countries – left bleeding on the battlefield.

Notes

1   The financial crisis started in the autumn of 2007 and still continues.
2   Saez, E. (2012). Striking it richer: The evolution of top incomes in the United States, http://Elsa.berkeley.edu/-saez/saez-USstopincomes-2010.pdf, accessed 2 March 2012.

3 G7: The Group of 7 consists of the seven major advanced economies: Canada, France, Germany, Italy, Japan, the United Kingdom, and the United States.
4 'Gulag' refers to the forced labour camps in the former Soviet Union. They were used as a tool of political repression, as a large number of the inmates were political prisoners, thus preventing opposing voices from speaking freely; cf. the Russian author Aleksander Solzhenitsyn's book *One Day in the Life of Ivan Denisovich*.
5 The Chinese currency.
6 The Norwegian newspaper *Aftenposten*, 25 October 2016.
7 *Aftenposten*, 26 October 2016.
8 The Danish newspaper *Politiken*, 17 September 2016.
9 Shiller cited by B. Wilkins in the US *Digital Journal*, 15 October 2013 (www.digital journal.com).
10 If a lie is repeated often enough, it will be believed. This is the basis of a Goebbelsian fact.
11 By theory we mean a system of propositions (Bunge, 1977). The statements we have presented here may be easily converted into propositions, thus explaining why we call this a theory.
12 This applies, for example, to the EU-Canada Trade Agreement (CETA) and the proposed EU-US Trade Agreement (TTIP).
13 G. Sargent cited Buffett in the *Washington Post*, 30 September 2011.
14 In Chile, for instance.
15 This was Trujillo in the Dominican Republic who became a burden. Trujillo was assassinated in 1961.
16 https://no.wikipedia.org/wiki/Irak-krigen, accessed 22 October 2016.
17 https://no.wikipedia.org/wiki/Irak-krigen, accessed 22 October 2016.
18 *Aftenposten*, 10 October 2016.
19 This comparison was made in the *New York Times*, February 1978 (in Chomsky, 2015a: 419, note 55).
20 The Russian Revolution took place in 1917.
21 In the field of psychology, Pavlov demonstrated stimulus-response in an experiment using dogs.
22 www.huffingtonpost.co.uk/ioan-marc-jones/owen-jones-establishment_b_5793868.html, accessed 22 October 2016.
23 G. Sargent cited Buffett in the *Washington Post*, 30 September 2011.
24 It should also be noted here that this view was shared by Lenin and Leninist ideology. It was the leaders of the communist movement that would lead the great masses to a better society that they themselves were unable to comprehend.
25 Interesting in this context is how the pope and Christian priests submitted obediently to Hitler before and during World War II (Johannessen, 2016: 44, see note 19 with references to "Hitler's pope").
26 G. Sargent cites Buffett in the *Washington Post*, 30 September 2011.
27 http://nyheder.tv2.dk/politik/2016-09-23-33000-danskere-rammes-af-kontanthjaelpsloftet-1-oktober.
28 *Politiken*, 23 October 2016.

References

Ariely, D. (2009). *Predictable irrational: The hidden forces that shape our decisions*, Harper, New York.

Azmat, G., Manning, A. & Van Reenen, J. (2012). Privatization and the decline of the labour's share: International evidence from network industries, *Economica*, 79:470–492.

Barrat, J. (2015). *Our final invention*, St. Martin's Griffin, London.

Bartels, L. (2008). *Unequal democracy*, Princeton University Press, Princeton.

Bauman, Z. (2013). *Does the richness of the few benefit us all?*, Polity, Cambridge.

Bunge, M. (1977). *Treatise on basic philosophy*. Vol. 3. Ontology I: The furniture of the world. Dordrecht, Holland: D. Reidel.

Case, S. (2016). *The third wave*, Simon & Schuster, New York.

Chomsky, N. (1999). *Profit over people*, Seven Stories Press, New York.

Chomsky, N. (2002). *Media control*, Seven Stories Press, New York.

Chomsky, N. (2012). *How the world works*, Hamish Hamilton, New York.

Chomsky, N. (2014). *Year 501: The conquest continues*, Haymarket Books, Chicago.

Chomsky, N. (2015). *Masters of mankind*, Penguin, London.

Chomsky, N. (2015a). *The Washington connection and third world fascism*, Pluto Press, New York.

Chomsky, N. (2016). *Who rules the world*, Hamish Hamilton, London.

Chomsky, N. (2016a). *Profit over people: War against people*, Piper, Berlin.

Coggan, P. (2011). *Paper promises: Money, debt and the new world order*, Allen Lane, New York.

Dorling, D. (2013). Fairness and the changing fortunes of people in Britain, *Journal of the Royal Statistical Society, A*, 176:1 (at dannydorling.org).

Dorling, D. (2015). *Inequality and the 1%*, Verso, London.

Ferguson, T. (1995). *Golden rule: The investment theory of part competition and the logic of money-driven political systems*, University of Chicago Press, Chicago.

Ferguson, T. & Rogers, J. (1981). *Hidden election*, Random House, New York.

Freeland, C. (2013). *Plutocrats: The rise of the new superrich*, Penguin, London.

Friedman, M. (2002). *Capitalism and freedom*, University of Chicago Press, Chicago.

Gaskarth, J. (Red.). (2015). *China, India and the future of international society*, Rowman & Littlefield, London.

Gilens, M. (2010). *Affluence and influence*, Princeton University Press, Princeton.

Gribb, J., Hood, A., Joyce, R. & Phillips, D. (2013). *Living standards, poverty and inequality in the UK*, Institute for Fiscal Studies, Report R81, pp. 30–45.

Hanson, R. (2016). *The age of EM: Work, love and life when robots rule the world*, Oxford University Press, Oxford.

Hines, C. (2000). *Localization*, Routledge, London.

Janis, I. (1982). *Groupthink*, Houghton Mifflin, New York.

Johannessen, J.-A. (2016). *Pauline Christianity versus the Christian faith*, Create Space, New York.

Jones, O. (2015). *The establishment*, Penguin, London.

Krugman, P. (2017). *Doughnut economics: Seven ways to think like a 21st-century economist*, Random House Business, New York.

Le Bon, G. (2014). *The crowd*, Aristeus Books, London.

Longerich, P. (2015). *Goebbels*, Vintage, London.

Macdonald, R. (2012). *Genesis of the financial crisis*, Palgrave, London.

McChesney, R. W. (2016). Introduction, in Chomsky, N. *Profit over people: War against people*, Piper, Berlin, p. 19.

McGill, K. (2016). *Global inequality*, University of Toronto Press, Toronto.

Miller, M. C. (2005). Introduction, in Bernays, E. *Propaganda*, IG Publishing, New York.

Monbiot, G. (2004). *The age of consent*, Harper, London.

OECD. (2002). *Preparing for the world summit: Some information about sustainable development*, Paris.

Piketty, T. (2014). *Capital in the twenty-first century*, The Belknap Press of Harvard University Press, Boston.

Piketty, T. (2016). *Chronicles: On our troubled times*, Viking, London.

Raskin, M. (2015). Foreword, in Chomsky, N. *Masters of mankind*, Penguin, London, pp. 9–19.

Saez, E. (2012). *Striking it richer: The evolution of top incomes in the United States*, http:// Elsa.berkeley.edu/-saez/saez-USstopincomes-2010.pdf. March 2, 2012.

Shipler, D. (2005). *The working poor*, Vintage, New York.

Smith, A. (1976). (first published in 1776) *The wealth of nations*, Clarendon Press, Oxford.

Standing, G. (2014). *The precariat: The new dangerous class*, Bloomsbury Academic, New York.

Standing, G. (2014a). *A precariat charter*, Bloomsbury, London.

Standing, G. (2016). *The corruption of capitalism*, Biteback Publishing, London.

Stiglitz, J. (2013). *The price of inequality*, Penguin, New York.

Stiglitz, J. (2016). *The great divide*, Penguin, New York.

Swider, S. (2015). *Building China: Informal work and the new*, Ilr Press, London.

Varoufakis, Y. (2015). *The global minotaur*, Zed Books, London.

Wilkin, S. (2016). *Wealth secrets of the 1%: The truth about money, markets and multi-millionaires*, Sceptre, London.

Wilkinson, R. & Pickett, K. (2009). *The spirit level: Why greater equality makes societies stronger*, Bloomsbury Press, London.

2 Robotization and the dissolution of the middle class

Introduction

For most of history, there was no middle class (Piketty, 2014: vv). The emergence of the middle class in the 19th century was a consequence of industrialization.

The traditional view, long held by economists, was based on Kuznets' curve, that is that inequalities increase to a certain level and then decrease as per capita income rises. This seemed to apply, for example, in the United States where 'everyone' in the 1960s and 1970s considered themselves middle class (Freeland, 2013: xii). However, at the end of the 1970s the wealthy began to overtake the middle class. By the start of the 2000s, a phenomenon had developed in OECD[1] countries whereby the super-rich had come to constitute a separate elite and the middle class had begun to be eroded (Bauman, 2013). A spanner had appeared in the works of so-called trickle-down economics[2] (Eagleton-Pierce, 2016; Harvey, 2007).

Through the First, Second, and Third Industrial Revolutions, the middle class has been a mainstay of change and an advocate of capitalism (Petras & Veltmeyr, 2011). Simultaneously with the growth of the precariat (Standing, 2014) in the Fourth Industrial Revolution, something is happening to the middle class. To a large extent, the middle class has been associated with management, control, and coordination functions in the economy. If these functions can be taken over by robots, then the most important functions of the middle class will have less significance.

An important driving force for the transformation of the middle class is robotization (the new information and communication technology), along with the growth of global technological platforms that make it simple and almost cost-free to start up new businesses without the traditional control functions (OECD, 2014). Having a middle-class job no longer guarantees a middle-class lifestyle (Schwab, 2016: 93). According to Schwab (2016: 93), the defining features of the middle class are:

1 Education
2 Health
3 Salary
4 Ownership of a house, apartment or other property.

An important development is that salaries will no longer be linked to the level of education (Gupta et al., 2016). This will quickly lead to the disappearance of the dream of a middle-class lifestyle. When being highly educated no longer guarantees either a job or a good income, expectations regarding both a future education and a high-quality lifestyle will change (Gupta et al., 2016). Another development is that middle-class children are becoming downwardly mobile – that is they have lower position and status than their parents (Monbiot, 2016).[3] Yet another point is that the welfare state has not brought about economic equality in Europe. Quite the contrary: economic inequality has increased during the period from the 1980s until today. This is the case in both Europe and the United States (McGill, 2016).

In addition, there is a direct connection between parents' education and their children's education: "The children of early retirees always become early retirees, and even the dimmest children of academics become academics."[4] While robots are taking over the jobs of the middle class, among others, this economic inequality is increasing (Pilger, 2016). This is leading to major social changes, with many people in the middle class ending up in insecure and poorly paid jobs. Equality of opportunity is not the same thing as equality, just as equality of opportunity is not the same thing as equality of results.

In Asia, however, the middle class is growing by approximately 150 million people every year. In 2016, 3.2 billion people were categorized as members of the middle class.[5] The decline of the middle class is thus a Western phenomenon. It is this Western phenomenon that we investigate in this chapter.

The question that we explore below is as follows:

HOW ARE ROBOTS AFFECTING THE MIDDLE CLASS?

We have summarized the introduction in Figure 2.1, which also shows how we have structured this chapter.

Robotization and social changes

First, we describe the trend associated with the question under discussion. Thereafter we analyze and discuss the phenomenon.

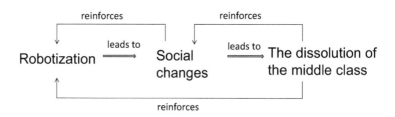

Figure 2.1 The dissolution of the middle class

Description

Robotization, digitization, and informats[6] are influencing how we think about ourselves and how we relate to others (Floridi, 2014: vi). Nanotechnology will soon enable us to exercise remote control over activities in our homes and workplaces. 'Singularity' – which is when the processing power of computers equals that of the human brain – is also just around the corner (Kurzweil, 2006). Soon this new technology will take over industrial business structures where middle managers previously managed workers' activities. Accordingly, the need for these middle-management positions will decline. One of the consequences will be that these functions will no longer need to be controlled by people. It is precisely these people who formed the backbone of the middle class. Accordingly, technology has a direct influence on the future of the middle class.

Among other things, informats are making it possible to manage, monitor, and influence processes and activities on a global scale. As a result, technology is not only affecting our lives but also how we think about our own lives and those of others (Sennett, 2013). Robotization – which we are using as an umbrella term for this new technology – is not only changing social structures but is also affecting both economic inequality and the complexity of the knowledge with which we surround ourselves. Taken together, these two factors will also affect our identity and our culture (Floridi, 2011).

For those people who see their jobs and positions disappearing and who no longer have the same expectations of the 'good life' for their children's future as they had for themselves, the new technology will be viewed as a threat and risk factor (Srinivasa, 2017). For others who have lighter work and who have the opportunity to do the work where it suits them best, the new technology will be viewed as advantageous.

For the millions who make up the precariat (Standing, 2014; Johnson, 2014), the new technology will be perceived as both an opportunity and a threat. Similar to previous technological revolutions, it is not so much the technology that will be the crucial factor determining the state of things but rather how the surplus generated by the new technology is distributed (Weinberger, 2011; Susskind & Susskind, 2015). Thus a key question is, how can we ensure that the benefits provided by new technology can benefit the many and not just the few?

The combustion engine and electricity were crucial to the development of the industrial revolution. Robotization, digitization, informats and the internet are directly linked to the development of the Fourth Industrial Revolution.[7] While the middle class may be viewed as emerging due to the first three industrial revolutions, the Fourth Industrial Revolution will lead to its dissolution (Castells, 2014: v–vi).

Most people are aware of the fact that the new technology is shifting society's 'tectonic plates.' The erosion of the middle class and its future dissolution is just one of these tectonic plates that has been put into motion. The precariat is another such tectonic plate. Extreme economic inequality is a third tectonic plate that is affecting social developments. In other words, society as we know it today is undergoing revolutionary changes. However, this is not so much a national, political, and social revolution such as those of history: the American Revolution (triggered in Boston in 1773), the French Revolution (triggered in 1789), the Russian October Revolution of 1917, and the Chinese Revolution of 1949. It is rather a global revolution with economic, social, political, and cultural consequences. Figuratively, this revolution may be likened to an explosion in slow motion. It may also be likened to the first agricultural revolution (8000 BC) and the first industrial revolution of about 250 years ago.

What is the alternative to the new technology? To turn back the clock to an industrial age that no longer exists? A more logical alternative would be to utilize the new technology globally so that everyone reaps the advantages of the technological and social revolution taking place. If we do this, the new technology can become a social mechanism for freedom for the many, instead of economic overabundance of the few (Mason, 2015; McGill, 2016).

The fear that machines will take over jobs and change social structures is nothing new. During the early days of industrialization at the beginning of the 1800s, the textile workers of the Luddite movement destroyed newly introduced machines in the textile industry with the aim of protecting their own jobs. In the short term, many jobs were lost because of the new technology. However, in the longer term, the machines created new jobs, increased productivity, and resulted in better pay conditions for workers overall. The new technology of the 1700s and 1800s created social changes and transformed social structures. Industrialization spawned both the working class and the middle class.

Robotization is bringing about the dissolution of the old middle class but promoting a new middle class that safeguards the ownership interests of an ever-smaller and richer upper class. The social changes we are witnessing thus lead to dissolution of the old middle class, creating a new and smaller middle class of highly paid leaders, as well as promoting the development of a plutocracy consisting of 1% of the population (Pilger, 2016).

The technological developments from the 1700s up until today improved the economic conditions of all the social classes in the industrialized world. Urbanization has increased, and social conditions, institutions, education, health, and social mobility have all been improved (Savage, 2015). However, there have also been setbacks. Some regions and communities have been become economic backwaters, and some groups have been excluded from the general increase in prosperity (Srinivasa, 2017). Yet despite these setbacks, technological developments have led to economic progress for most people. It is this thinking that lies behind the optimism in new technological developments regarding robots, informats, artificial intelligence, digitization, and so forth.

The thinking of the technology optimists is historically rooted. During the industrial revolution, superfluous agricultural workers moved from rural areas to industrial jobs in the towns. In turn, their children and grandchildren moved from industrial jobs to service and knowledge jobs. These transitions led to short-term employment challenges. However, the new jobs were better paid and consisted of lighter work, resulting in less physical drudgery than before. In order to cope with the major changes that came as a result of new technology, mass university education was introduced so that all those with ability were given the opportunity to educate themselves and find employment in better jobs. In this way, demands for new skills were continually met by various types of university study programmes.

However, something began to happen in the 1970s and 1980s: productivity increased, but wages did not increase accordingly. This mismatch became more apparent after the economic crisis of 2007–2008. This situation led to owners of capital getting richer, while there was no noticeable increase in the living standards of wage earners (Piketty, 2014). This was the case in both the United States and Europe. Just before that, something unexpected happened: starting around 2000, many new jobs were created, but the vast majority of them were part-time jobs (Ford, 2016: x–xi). These part-time jobs and contract work have become the hallmarks of the new precariat (Johnson, 2014).

At the same time, not many new full-time jobs were created, and as mentioned wages have not risen in line with productivity, resulting in a sharp increase in economic inequality. The owners of capital have taken an increasingly larger share of the profits of economic growth, while wage earners have benefitted to a lesser extent (Piketty, 2014: 1–15). Work and the new technology have reached a point where they no longer mutually support each other. The new technology is increasingly utilized as an income source for capital (Monbiot, 2016). Robotization, digitization, and information technology have reinforced this development. The people who have ideologically supported capital profits are increasingly disappearing; the old middle class is being dissolved by the technological advances that robotization leads to.

What is happening at the same time is that industrial jobs are not only being replaced by cheap labour from low-cost countries, but industrial workers are also being replaced by robotization which is detrimental to middle-class jobs.

The dreams, expectations, class mobility, new positioning, dominance, and control of others that were all part of the old middle class have almost become history over a 50-year period from the 1970s and 1980s up until today. The old middle class is in the process of being dissolved (James, 2008; Mills, 2008). Like the phoenix, the new middle class has risen from the 2007–2008 crisis. The old middle class literally emerged from the factories, universities, and commercial activities; this social class consisted of merchants, factory foremen, teachers, doctors, lawyers, entrepreneurs, and so forth. In 1951, Mills (2008) called them "white-collar workers." They could be seen all around the world going to their offices, wearing suits and ties and carrying umbrellas. Their ideology included obedience and hard work, and they demanded the same of the people they controlled and had power over. These are the people that Max Weber describes and conceptualized in his bureaucracy models and in his ideas about Protestant ethics, obedience, and hard work. However, this thinking changed around the 1980s with the development of neoliberalism and the 'winner takes all' principle. In this context, the winners were those who owned capital (McGill, 2016).

The financial crisis that started in the autumn of 2007 greatly affected millions of workers worldwide. At the same time, we saw the largest flow ever of income to those working on Wall Street in 2009; for instance, Goldman Sachs paid its employees a record average of $600,000 (Hacker & Pierson, 2010: 2–3). These employees represent the picture that emerges of the new middle class – those working with finance capital, top executives and others in well-paid key positions. On the other hand, after 2007 the wage trends of the old middle class do not bear comparison. However, the picture becomes distorted when we know that public funds and the central banks in the Western world made it possible for the new middle class to live their opulent lives while the workers and the old middle class saw both their employment opportunities and income diminish (Dorling, 2015: 15–35).

The emergence of a super-rich upper class, a small rich middle class, and the pulverization of the old middle class started with the stagflation of the 1970s and gained momentum with the neoliberalist ideology of the 1980s. Robotization and the financial crisis triggered in the autumn of 2007 reinforced these developments (Johannessen, 2016: 128–134).

Thus, there is a hyper-concentration of wealth: the 1% class at the top of the prosperity pyramid gets away with the largest share of value creation (Savage, 2015). Hence, the new oligarchs not only dominate the Russian economy but also the economy of the West to a great extent. This rich man's empire or plutocracy is synonymous with the feudal capitalism that is emerging. The old middle class, with its management, control, and coordination functions, is not effective in feudal capitalism as it was in industrial capitalism. At the same time, the labour market has also become more uncertain (Sennett, 1999, 2003, 2009, 2013; Standing, 2014). One might say that the old middle class was based on a low-tech economy, while the new middle class, consisting of much fewer people, is based on a high-tech economy where robots, artificial intelligence, digitization, and globalization are elements.

One of the consequences of this development is that competence requirements are changing. This can partly be explained by the fact that robots and artificial intelligence will take over many of the activities that the middle class previously carried out, or that their services will no longer be in demand.

Thus, the opposition will not be between those who have a vocational education or other type of higher education and those who don't, but between the few at the top who take the largest share of the cake and the rest who have to fight over the crumbs (Srinivasa, 2017). The few at the top have also managed to get the middle class to take all the risks arising from technological change. For instance, the middle class has taken on a very large debt burden, which has given more and more people work because the debt has been used for the purchase of housing, cars, transportation and travel, and consumption of various kinds (Bauman, 2013). However, when the debt bubble bursts, either under its own weight, due to an international crisis, or by interest rate hikes, then we will see the consequences of this debt lending. Those who have earned and still earn on this debt lending are the 1% at the top of the economic pyramid (Hacker & Pierson, 2010: 13–14). Since the 1980s, the 1% has greatly increased its wealth, while income increases have largely stopped for the middle class and the working class (Dorling, 2015).

The neoliberal mindset from the 1980s up until today has been based on a trickle-down economy: the idea that if the rich get richer, then others get richer too. However, the truth is rather that there has been a 'trickle-up economy,' where the wealthy have grown richer while others haven't (Bauman, 2013; Chomsky, 2016, 2016a).

The financial crisis of 2007–2008 resulted in a drop in American middle-class income – the first time this had happened in American history. This also resulted in an increase in the numbers of the lower middle class and a corresponding decrease in the middle and the upper class (Aghai, 2014: ix). In addition, from 2007 to the present day, there has been little if any movement upwards on the economic ladder for the middle class. In reality, this means that the middle class is being pushed downwards towards a lower income position from which it will be very difficult to emerge. Thus, they have been locked into a 'trickle-down economy,' which is part and parcel of the neoliberal ideology that has been implemented (Petras & Veltmeyr, 2011; Harvey, 2007; Eagleton-Pierce, 2016).

The dissolution of the middle class will not occur overnight but will develop as a slow, evolutionary process, directly linked to technological developments. However, the social changes will not only be due to technological innovations. Among other things, from the 1980s onwards, several traditional middle-class jobs have been outsourced to low-income areas. This development may partly explain some of the poor income development of the middle class. One of the consequences is an increasing middle-class debt. From 1971 to 2012, debt growth increased by 1,700% (Aghai, 2014: 2). By the autumn of 2007 (when the financial crisis was triggered), mortgage debt had grown so large that it resulted in many being forced to leave their homes (when housing prices fell). The result was a financial and social crisis which we are still feeling the consequences of today. In the United States, there was an increase in poverty, with about 100 million either in poverty or in the zone just above it; this also affected 39% of all children in the United States (Aghai, 2014: 2). One might be tempted to say that the financial crisis of 2007–2008 inflicted a death blow on the traditional middle class. On the other hand, a new middle class is emerging, characterized by high income. The people in this group, as mentioned above, may be said to be the upper part of the middle class. These are the highly paid senior executives, highly educated academics, lawyers, economists, engineers, and so forth.

The dissolution of the traditional middle class has occurred while the new middle class has emerged in the global economy. In addition to this, a traditional middle class is increasing in China, for example (Gaskarth, 2015; Swider, 2015).

Analysis and discussion

Artificial intelligence, intelligent algorithms and informats have already been developed so that many of the typical work activities of the middle class have already been rendered redundant (Abd, 2017). On the other hand, there are some cases where businesses have introduced robots but still increased their numbers of employees.[8] However, this is rather the exception to the rule (Bleuer et al.,

2017; Brynjolfsson & McAfee, 2014). For instance, in the future many jobs will quickly disappear in travel agencies, law firms, data analysis companies, journalism, transport, computer programming, and even more in finance and banking, This is what some call "technology-led unemployment" (Ford, 2016). Yet this predicted increase in unemployment is by no means governed by a law of nature. If working hours are reduced sharply and more workers share the work, there is nothing to indicate that technology-led unemployment is something that can be avoided. Nevertheless, if we do not share the value creation created by the new technology, unemployment will sharply increase in most social layers.

However, not all areas of employment will suffer; for instance, there will be a transition from permanent full-time jobs to part-time jobs and contract work (Standing, 2014; Johnson, 2014). This will lead to many in the middle class ending up in the precariat on part-time contracts, in worse jobs than they had before (Case, 2016; Davenport & Kirby, 2005).

As a rule, it will be the relatively well-paid middle-class jobs that disappear while the new jobs will be part-time (Davidow & Malone, 2014). The other tendency is that upper-middle-class jobs will increase (Casselman, 2013).

In some situations, workers will need to have more than one job to get by (Shipler, 2005). It might be said that technology will be a decisive contributing factor in the dissolution of the middle class in the West. As mentioned, there will also be a tendency for full-time employment to be reduced, and in many cases, workers will be hired on so-called zero-hour contracts. This was also the case for many workplaces in the interwar period. Workers turned up for work, and the lucky few were picked out to work for a few hours or days but without any expectation of permanent employment (Wacquant, 2009, 2009a). The polarization of work described here – involving a large part of the workforce being hired on contracts and poorly paid, and a small highly educated part of the workforce being well paid – are not the only factors that will impact employment conditions. There is also a third factor that will drive this polarization of working life. Robots, informats, and artificial intelligence will greatly affect and change the working conditions of both the highly educated and contract workers (Weinberger, 2011). The loss of middle-class jobs is not the result of an 'overall plan,' as part of 'a war' against the middle class, rather the contrary. It is the small and major economic crises that force companies and organizations to focus on costs and productivity (Brynjolfsson & McAfee, 2014). Consequently, it might be said that the middle class is pressed on at least two fronts: the new technology and economic crises. Both the new technology and the economic crises will come in cascades (Johannessen, 2016). Therefore, the pressure on the middle class will not be constant, but will occur periodically and at a very high temperature (Ford, 2016: 52).

What are the new aspects of the technological developments we are witnessing today, in relation to the First, Second, and Third Industrial Revolutions, characterized by agricultural machinery, the steam engine, the combustion engine, the assembly line, the electric motor, the car, the computer, and the internet? The first thing we can establish is that it is different this time around. However, what is different, and how does this affect the middle class? In the First and Second

Industrial Revolutions, there was a demand for people who could govern, control, communicate, and coordinate production activities. These people became part of the middle-manager stratum in businesses and organizations. These middle managers formed the backbone of the growing middle class. This middle class saw it as a priority to give their children a good education so that they could become economists, doctors, nurses, priests, teachers, lawyers, engineers, and so forth (Davidow & Malone, 2014). This development further strengthened the middle class. However, in the Third Industrial Revolution, when computers and the internet were used in businesses and organizations, productivity increased as a result of the new technology and the new management tools that controlled and coordinated production.

In the Fourth Industrial Revolution, technological developments resulted in some of the management, control, and coordination functions being automated and replacing the activities of middle managers. This resulted in a significant increase in productivity, but now without the need of more employees.

In addition to the management, control, and coordination functions being taken over by the new technology, robots, informats, artificial intelligence, and intelligent algorithms, the new technology targeted the information-using functions of organizations. If we imagine organizations and businesses as comprising production- and information-using components, then during the First, Second, and partly the Third Industrial Revolutions, the production component became highly automated due to technological developments, while in the Fourth Industrial Revolution the information-using component is becoming highly automated due to new technological developments.

The new technology will result in the traditional pyramid form of businesses, institutions, and organizations being blown to pieces. After the dust has settled, what is left behind will be something completely different. One may be tempted to figuratively imagine a phoenix rising from the ashes,[9] that is some kind of re-creation in the future of what existed in the past. However, this will not be the case: the new organizational form will be completely different and not resemble the old one. A more appropriate analogy would be that of autonomous LEGO blocks – in other words, autonomous units that manufacture and distribute products and services according to some very basic simple rules. These basic rules are mainly oriented around costs, quality, expertise, and innovation. The LEGO blocks will be controlled from centres in the big cities (Florida, 2017), and according to a logic of costs, expertise, and innovation, some of these blocks will be located in global areas such as China, some in Bangalore, India, others in South Africa, California, and so forth. The LEGO blocks, which may be small or large, gather close to the market to merge into the final product or service. In this way, the pyramid form will be blown into thousands of pieces and the production form that emerges will not be visible as such. The new organizational structure with its focal point in the big cities will have no need of middle managers to govern, control, and coordinate production or information. Robots, informats, and artificial intelligence will carry out the activities that were previously performed by middle managers and employees. This time, the disruptions caused by new technology will be completely different from before, because it is the information-using component of businesses and organizations that is being informatized and where the disruptions are taking place. While the First and Second Industrial Revolutions were mainly responsible for the creation of the middle class, the Fourth Industrial Revolution will to a great extent be responsible for its dissolution, as there will be no need for middle management among other things. As mentioned, the pyramid form of businesses and organizations will also crumble.

While a great number of middle-class jobs have largely been concerned with controlling, collecting, and analyzing information for senior management, this can now be done by intelligent algorithms, artificial intelligence, robots, and informats. What will then happen to many of the employees in middle-management and administrative positions? These employees formed the backbone of the middle class. In the future, using the new technology, senior management will be able to perform many of the above tasks associated with middle management and administration today. These developments will result in organizations changing not only content but also form. This will involve a transition from the traditional pyramid form to something resembling a pancake. The pancake symbolizes the front-line focus, that is those who are in direct contact with the customer – the student, the patient, the users, and so forth – which is essential for value creation. In practice, this means that the intermediaries represented by middle managers and administrative positions will eventually disappear.

If we take an abstract view of this analysis using LEGO blocks, a few simple basic rules, and a front-line focus, then James G. Miller's theory (1978) may provide an explanation of what is happening. Miller says that a viable system needs 20 processes to survive. There are nine processes that make up the production system and 11 processes that make up the information component of all systems, such as in an organization. In Figure 2.2 we have visualized these processes.

All the processes in the production system are automated or distributed according to a cost, quality, competence, and innovation logic. Most of the processes in the administrative system are being robotized in one way or another. The result is that the pyramid and its associated social structures will be dissolved and replaced by autonomous LEGO blocks.

When more and more middle managers lose their secure and predictable incomes, which tied them to the middle classes, it will take some time before they realize they have been 'declassed' and no longer belong to those who previously perceived themselves as privileged. Many of these people will fall into the precariat (Standing, 2014; Johnson, 2014). Perhaps they will still feel that they belong to the middle classes, with its ideology that everyone is "the author of their own success." With such a way of thinking, they will still ideologically support the upper classes. They will live for a period with this false consciousness and the hope of climbing back to the social class position they have lost. It is only when the precariat are able to identify themselves as a separate social class that the 'rebellion' will come, says Standing (2014).

A few from the old middle class will emerge as successful in the new era; these leading lights will buttress the false consciousness of the de-classed millions

"Pancake" organization   **LEGO block structure**

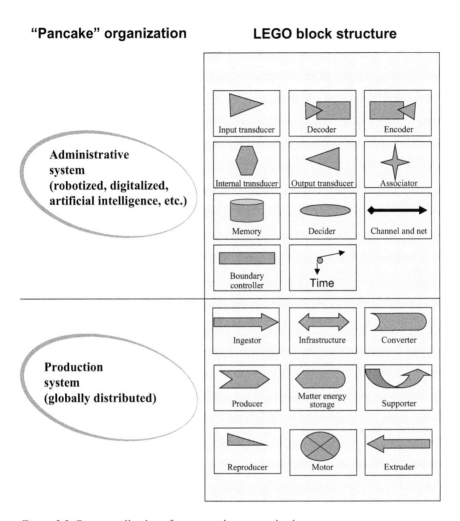

Figure 2.2 Conceptualization of processes in an organization

(Wacquant, 2009). It is the hope, the dream, the expectations that will hold the de-classed middle class in a false consciousness (Wacquant, 2009). However, there will be only a few people who will be able to take a place at the table of the rich. Most of the old middle class will fall into the precariat. It is only their hopes and dreams that will keep their false consciousness intact (Wacquant, 2007, 2009a).

Parts of the old middle class and their children will most likely be sucked into the ideology of being the author of their own success, that is becoming entrepreneurs and starting their own businesses so they can get rich, become powerful, and join society's rich elite (Savage, 2015). However, most people will realize that there is a downside to the dream of owning their own business. This is related to uncertainty – an uncertain income, which will make it difficult to plan having a family and, not least, plan for retirement. There is also great uncertainty linked to whether they will succeed with their projects – in reality, most will certainly fail. Therefore, the dream of starting your own business could be just that: a dream (Susskind & Susskind, 2015). As mentioned, the precariat will most likely attract the eroded and pulverized middle class. Hopes and dreams will disappear and a new class consciousness will eventually emerge, says Standing (2014). This new class consciousness will not evolve from the proletariat but from the new precariat. However, this will not be like the factory workers of the industrial age who joined together to form unions. The precariat are atomized, angry, and frustrated people – those who have seen their dreams and hopes crushed even though they may have completed medium- or long-term higher education programmes. This 'rebellion' will take the form of gang-like groups – packs of wolves attacking at random and in all directions (Johnson, 2014; Standing, 2014).

The few who succeed – those who build great wealth from two empty hands – will serve as role models for the many who fail. The mediocre – those who are only average at most things – will only have the hope, a smartphone, and a dream that tomorrow they will create the idea that will take them into the upper classes. However, the 99.99% will only have the hope, remain in the dream, and possibly live with this dream until departure from life brings them the equality they sought. Stories and narratives about the one who climbed from nothing to the top of the money pyramid after starting with only two empty hands will keep the hope and false consciousness alive for this group.

Will knowledge-based jobs be a way out for the middle class and their children? The new technology will probably first affect information- and knowledge-based jobs, as we have witnessed in the finance and banking systems (Savage, 2015). Furthermore, it is likely that many of the secure, permanent full-time jobs will become insecure and replaced by part-time contracts (Rojecki, 2016). The traditional wage earners from the factories of the 19th and 20th centuries may be replaced by a form of 'gig economy' – a type of 'on demand' economy – where small-scale entrepreneurs emerge and try to earn a living and supplement their income. We see this in businesses such as Airbnb, Uber, Etsy, Love Home Swap, TaskRabbit, and Onefinestay, to name a few. These small-scale entrepreneurs can be those who replace the mass production of the 1800s and 1900s. The technological revolution, with internet, smartphones, and so forth makes this development possible. The new businesses that are part of the 'peer-to-peer economy'[10] are completely different from, for example, Apple, BP, and similar major global businesses. Those who offer their services do not take on full-time jobs; their work activities only take up a small part of their time in their everyday lives, such as those who are active in Airbnb and similar peer-to-peer services. One is one's own boss in these work relationships, and this may be viewed as becoming a hidden source of income of the middle class when their jobs are eroded. For many in the middle class that create new jobs in this way, it will also mean that permanent and secure monthly salaries will disappear. When incomes become uncertain, attitudes and habits will also change. The two cars many families today own, may be replaced by a rental car scheme, where many share one car. It may become more economically viable to rent and share a house with others instead of owning a house. Several types of collective living solutions will also appear. In Denmark, alternatives to state-run retirement homes have emerged, such as the *Oldingekollektiv* (*oldekolle*), where older people live together in collectives.

Conclusion

The question we examined here was:

HOW ARE ROBOTS AFFECTING THE MIDDLE CLASS?

We have summarized the brief answer in Figure 2.3.

Explanation of the typology

We have divided this typology into two main axes that we believe will be decisive for many jobs that the middle class has performed in the past and, to some extent, will perform in the future. These are the requirement for formal competence and the requirement to be creative and innovative.

Those jobs that do not demand a high level of creativity and where the levels of competence required is relatively low are generally managerial and control jobs in businesses. These jobs will be taken over, and to a large extent have already been

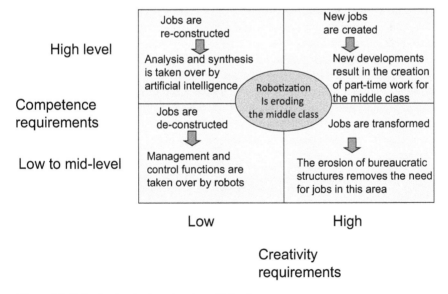

Figure 2.3 Robotization is changing the middle class

taken over, by digitized and robotic systems. These jobs are being deconstructed and are disappearing, even though the actual activities involved are not disappearing. In all likelihood, the activities are being performed by robots or informats in one form or another. The upside is the need for technicians who can maintain and design these robots and informats.

Those jobs that demand little creative focus but a high level of competence will be jobs that have been performed by highly competent, graduate knowledge workers. Examples here are lawyers, economists, technologists, and so forth. There will be less need for such jobs when intelligent algorithms and artificial intelligence are implemented in robots and informats. These are jobs where the ability to analyze and synthesize are the decisive factors. These jobs will be re-constructed and the functions will be performed by new technology. This will take a little longer than with the jobs that are being deconstructed, but it is only a question of time before these jobs are replaced by new technology. Of course, the upside is that technicians will be required to maintain these technologies, and technologists will be needed to design and develop them.

Those jobs that require a high level of creativity but only a low level of competence are listed in the typology in Figure 2.3 as jobs that will be transformed. These may be various kinds of service functions in the gig economy, where the peer-to-peer segment is creating small entrepreneurial businesses without the bureaucracy of middle management. This is where one may envisage middle-class people who have lost their secure jobs in pyramid organizations. When these organizations evolve into more 'pancake' and global LEGO-block style structures, demand for control and management functions will be minimized and in general taken over by robots, artificial intelligence, and digital solutions.

New jobs for the middle class will be created in areas that demand a high level of creativity and an extremely high level of competence. These are the innovative solutions that will create the new kind of creativity that has not existed in the world before. Some of these activities will put people from the middle class at the top of the income pyramid. Other examples of these creative new jobs will remain part-time activities that will create insecure incomes. It is in this segment, however, where the opportunity lies to create a future for many of the children of the middle class. Here lies the hope, dream, and belief of a better future. At the same time, this is also the root of the idea that you are the author of your own success, which is what is preventing an uprising by the precariat against the plutocracy.

Notes

1 Organisation for Economic Co-operation and Development.
2 Trickle-down economics was the ideology adopted by Ronald Reagan and Margaret Thatcher.
3 The Danish newspaper *Politiken*, 21 March 2017.
4 The Danish newspaper *Information*, 7 April 2017.
5 The Norwegian newspaper *Aftenposten*, 3 May 2017. It cites a report from the Brookings Institution, a US think tank.

6 Here we define informats as robots that are linked with other robots in a global network, meaning that they always have access to the latest information and can act in accordance with it.
7 The First Industrial Revolution is associated with the introduction of the steam engine; the Second Industrial Revolution is associated with the combustion engine; the Third Industrial Revolution is associated with the computer.
8 The Norwegian newspaper, *Dagens Næringsliv*, 21 May 2017.
9 The phoenix rises from its own ashes after being consumed by flames.
10 *Guardian*, 23 May 2017.

References

Abd, K. K. (2017). *Intelligent scheduling of robotic flexible assembly cells*, Springer, London.
Aghai, V. (2014). *America's shrinking middle class*, Author House, Bloomington.
Bauman, Z. (2013). *Does the richness of the few benefit us all?*, Polity, London.
Bleuer, H., Bouri, M. & Mandada, F. C. (2017). *New trends in medical and service robots*, Springer, London.
Brynjolfsson, E. & McAfee, A. (2014). *The second machine age*, W. W. Norton & Company, New York.
Case, S. (2016). *The third wave*, Simon & Schuster, New York.
Casselman, B. (2013). Low pay clouds job growth, *Wall Street Journal*, 3 April.
Castells, M. (2014). Foreword, in Graham, M. & Dutton, W. H. (Eds.). *Society & the internet*, Oxford University Press, Oxford, pp. v–vi.
Chomsky, N. (2016). *Who rules the world*, Hamish Hamilton, London.
Chomsky, N. (2016a). *Profit over people: War against people*, Piper, Berlin.
Davenport, T.H. & Kirby, J. (2005). *Only humans need apply: Winners & losers in the age of smart machines*, Harper Business, New York.
Davidow, W. H. & Malone, M. C. (2014). What happens to society when robots replace workers, *Harvard Business Review*, 10 December.
Dorling, D. (2015). *Inequality and the 1%*, Verso, London.
Eagleton-Pierce, M. (2016). *Neoliberalism: The key concepts*, Routledge, London.
Florida, R. (2017). *The urban crises*, Oneworld Publication, New York.
Floridi, L. (2011). *The philosophy of information*, Oxford University Press, Oxford.
Floridi, L. (2014). *The 4th revolution*, Oxford University Press, Oxford.
Ford, M. (2016). *The rise of the robots: Technology and the threat of mass unemployment*, Oneworld, London.
Freeland, C. (2013). *Plutocrats: The rise of the new superrich*, Penguin, London.
Gaskarth, J. (Ed.). (2015). *China, India and the future of international society*, Rowman & Littlefield, London.
Gupta, S., Habjan, J. & Tutek, H. (2016). *Academic labour unemployment and global higher education: Neoliberal politics of funding and management*, Palgrave, London.
Hacker, J. S. & Pierson, P. (2010). *Winner-take-all politics*, Simon & Schuster, New York.
Harvey, D. (2007). *A brief history of neoliberalism*, Oxford University Press, Oxford.
James, L. (2008). *The middle class: A history*, Abacus, New York.
Johannessen, J.-A. (2016). *Innovation leads to economic crises: Explaining the bubble economy*, Palgrave, London.
Johnson, M. (2014). *Precariat, labour, work and politics*, Routledge, London.
Kurzweil, R. (2006). *The singularity is near*, Gerald Duckworth & Co Ltd., London.

Mason, P. (2015). *Postcapitalism: A guide to our future*, Allen Lane, London.

McGill, K. (2016). *Global inequality*, University of Toronto Press, Toronto.

Miller, J. G. (1978). *Living systems*, McGill, New York.

Mills, C. W. (2008). *White collar: The American middle class*, Oxford University Press, Oxford.

Monbiot, G. (2016). *How did we get into this mess*, Verso, London.

OECD. (2014). *Policy challenges for the next 50 years*, Brussels, OECD.

Petras, J. & Veltmeyr, H. (2011). *Beyond neoliberalism: A word to win*, Routledge, London.

Piketty, T. (2014). *Capital in the twenty-first century*, The Belknap Press of Harvard University Press, Boston.

Pilger, J. (2016). *The new rulers of the world*, Verso, London.

Rojecki, A. (2016). *America and the politics of insecurity*, John Hopkins University Press, New York.

Savage, M. (2015). *Social class in the 21st century*, Penguin, London.

Schwab, K. (2016). *The fourth industrial revolution*, World Economic Forum, Geneva.

Sennett, R. (1999). *The corrosion of character*, W. W. Norton, New York.

Sennett, R. (2003). *The fall of public man*, Penguin, New York.

Sennett, R. (2009). *The craftsman*, Penguin, New York.

Sennett, R. (2013). *Together*, Penguin, New York.

Shipler, D. (2005). *The working poor*, Vintage, New York.

Srinivasa, R. (2017). *Whose global village: Rethinking how technology shapes the world*, New York University Press, London.

Standing, G. (2014). *The precariat: The new dangerous class*, Bloomsbury Academic, New York.

Susskind, R. & Susskind, D. (2015). *The future of professions: How technology will transform the work of human experts*, Oxford University Press, Oxford.

Swider, S. (2015). *Building China: Informal work and the new*, Ilr Press, London.

Wacquant, L. (2007). *Urban outcast*, Polity, London.

Wacquant, L. (2009). *Punishing the poor*, Duke University Press, London.

Wacquant, L. (2009a). *Prisons of poverty*, University of Minnesota Press, New York.

Weinberger, D. (2011). *Too big to know: Rethinking knowledge now that the fact aren't the facts, experts are everywhere, and the smartest person in the room is the room*, Basic Books, New York.

3 'Men in suits' are promoting extreme economic inequality

Introduction

From an economic perspective, we are accustomed to thinking that increased labour productivity will reduce inequality and increase earned income. Piketty (2014: 51–52) has shown that neither of these assumptions is correct at the dawn of the Fourth Industrial Revolution. Piketty (2014: 39–72) also points out that unearned income has been greater than value creation would suggest. Put simply, this means that those who own capital will, as time goes on, become richer and richer compared with everyone else. When growth is rapid, this inequality is concealed because wage earners, pensioners, and recipients of welfare benefits also see their incomes increase.

The financial crisis that was triggered in 2007–2008 caused economic growth to stagnate. As a result, economic inequality became more visible. In the absence of intervention, this increase in economic inequality will in all probability continue (Bauman, 2013: 6–20). An effective way of reducing this economic inequality is to tax unearned income (Piketty, 2014: 113–199). The point is that few political parties adopt this policy because the official version is that economic inequality is good for everyone (Bauman, 2013).

What needs to be done to address this inequality is largely a political question. For example, lower tax on low-to-average earned income and higher tax on private capital would have an impact on this economic inequality (Piketty, 2014: 113–199). When economists discuss economic inequality as opposed to economic equality, they do so based on a subjective understanding about what is good, rather than on the basis of scholarly and objective economic fact (Bauman, 2013: 27–48; Piketty, 2014: 1–16).

Another example of this is the theory of supply-side economics, which was first advanced by the economist Robert Mundell[1] and put into practice by the Reagan administration in the United States and Margaret Thatcher in the United Kingdom. Supporters of supply-side economics argue, among other things, that lowering taxes for wage earners will encourage people to work harder, which in turn will promote value creation and higher tax revenues. In other words: lower taxes lead to higher tax revenues. Proponents of supply-side economics used the same reasoning to justify reducing taxes on people with private capital. They argued that reducing tax on private capital would encourage people to invest more, which would have the effect of increasing government revenues since more investment would create more jobs.[2] This economic ideology is the conservative economic bible. Several studies have shown, however, that reducing taxes has little impact on economic growth, which was (and is) the whole point of this ideology.[3] There is a lack of objective scholarly results to support this approach, which has been shown in several empirical scholarly studies to constitute political ideology rather than economic fact.[4]

Economic growth is promoted by completely different factors, including new technology, innovation, competence development, and organization, something which economists showed in the American economy over the course of a century – including the Nobel Laureate in Economics, Robert Solow (1956).[5] People with private incomes are interested, however, in maintaining the myth that lower taxes are in everyone's interests, while in reality they benefit only those who pay less tax, who in all likelihood are the highest earners and/or those with private capital.

Extreme economic inequality has existed ever since it became possible to accumulate wealth (Wolff & De-Shalit, 2007). We are limiting this investigation to the threshold of the Fourth Industrial Revolution, whereby robots, informats,[6] and artificial intelligence will take over many of the functions relating to value creation. Our primary focus in the study is industrial countries within the OECD.

The question investigated in this chapter is as follows:

WHAT IS PROMOTING EXTREME ECONOMIC INEQUALITY?

In order to address this question, we investigate three sub-questions:

> RQ1: Why does extreme economic inequality exist?
> RQ2: What social mechanisms are sustaining extreme economic inequality?
> RQ3: Why is economic equality preferable?

This introduction is visualized in Figure 3.1, which also illustrates how we have structured this chapter.

Economics as ideology

The question we investigate here is as follows: why does extreme economic inequality exist?

This question is related to the distribution of value creation. First, we describe why extreme economic inequality exists. Thereafter, we analyze and discuss the phenomenon. Finally, in this part, we develop a sub-conclusion which answers the sub-research question.

Description

We know that top executives earn enormous salaries compared to most wage earners. In 2016, Credit Suisse CEO Tidjane Thiam earned NOK 101 million in

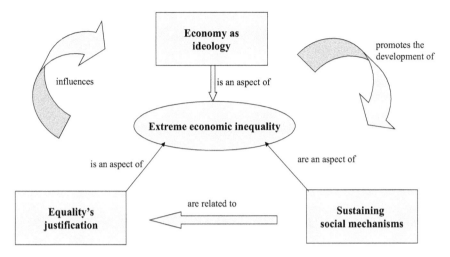

Figure 3.1 Extreme economic inequality

salary and bonuses, even though the bank itself lost billions.[7] The belief that it will benefit everybody if a few people earn vast sums of money contributes to maintaining inequality. The debate on the distribution of wealth that is created, and its consequences, has been based largely on ideology rather than data. It is with Piketty's (2014) study that we see for the first time an explanation of wealth distribution that is based on a large quantity of data. Prior to Piketty's research, the field has been dominated mainly by arguments based on ideology.

Not surprisingly, the Marxist argument has been that private property rights leads to the accumulation and centralization of capital. On the other hand, classical and neoclassical economists have argued that competition promotes equal distribution of value creation.[8]

However, neither the classical economists nor Karl Marx used a particularly large database to support their theories and proposed policies regarding economic inequality. Such data was not available until Kuznets conducted his research in 1953 (Kuznets, 1953).

What we do know is that technological innovations, economic growth, and increasing productivity have hampered, if not reduced, capital accumulation and concentration of capital (Piketty, 2014: 10). What we often hear is that economic growth is like a rising tide that lifts all boats. This aphorism is associated with the so-called Kuznets curve, which suggests that industrialization first led to greater inequality, and then reduced this economic inequality (Kuznets, 1953). The rising tide aphorism and Kuznets' data are striking. However, Piketty (2014: 10–13; 581, note 15) expresses that Kuznets' rising tide theory may be likened to a fairy tale, and cannot be validated by a review of his data. Kuznets was aware of such a criticism and stated explicitly in his research that greater future economic equality cannot be interpreted specifically from the data, but rather that this was an assumption (Kuznets, 1953: 24–26). However, the Kuznets curve has later been understood as if it represented fact-based knowledge; that is, that economic growth is like a rising tide that lifts all boats. Political arguments and policy measures regarding the development of economic equality/inequality are largely based on this curve. This was also a main intention of Kuznets (1953: 24–26). The Marxist theory that capitalism will eventually destroy itself due to increasing inequality became less politically viable with the acceptance of the optimistic interpretation and assumption suggested by Kuznets' curve.

However, what we do know from the data between 1980 up until today is that some people have become extremely rich, while many have become poorer; others have extremely difficult and unpredictable working conditions (Weeks, 2014; Standing, 2014; Piketty, 2015). Nevertheless, in low-cost countries such as China, developments have taken a different direction. The number of rich has increased, and the middle class has also grown in numbers and wealth, while low-paid workers have also improved their lives (Jones, 2015).

Analysis and discussion

The Kuznets curve illustrates the hypothesis that economic growth leads first to greater economic inequality and then to greater economic equality (Kuznets, 1953, 1955). However, other theorists, including Piketty (2014: 14–15), have presented differing analyses. Piketty shows that in all probability, the economic trend from 1980 onwards has led only to greater economic inequality, even though this has been a period of economic growth. If Piketty's analysis is correct, we can no longer argue that economic inequality will be reduced if we simply leave it up to the market to even things out.

Milanovic (2016: 46–118) attempted to save Kuznets' hypothesis by introducing the concept of 'Kuznets' waves.' However, the problem with Milanovic's analysis is that he presents historical data as if the past will fall into the same cycle in the future (cf. Milanovic, 2016: 58: Fig. 2.4). The idea that war and crises lead to greater levelled-out equality is nothing new. However, it only shows that when the rich suffer loss, the poor suffer from distress; but there is a difference between loss and distress; even although the average economic inequality may be diminished through war and crisis, which Milanovic (2016: 46–118) empirically points out. Another objection to Milanovic's claim that "I introduce the concept of Kuznets waves or cycles" (Milanovic, 2016: 4) is that this had already been done by Ernst Mandel 52 years earlier (Mandel, 1964, 1980).

After the 1980s, economic inequality has increased considerably in developed countries, as pointed out by Piketty (2014), Stiglitz (2002, 2012, 2015), and Weeks (2014), among others. An important point made by Piketty (2014, 2015) is that you cannot leave it to the market to level out economic inequality. It is rather the political system that needs to intervene and tackle the problem of economic inequality.

Since the 1980s and up until today, economic inequality has increased due to deliberate political policies. Ideas concerning what is just and unjust have changed throughout history. Since the 1980s, after the introduction of neoliberalism, it has been a common perception that the individual is responsible for his or her own actions and the consequences of those actions. When people in positions of power promote neoliberal ideology, resulting in the implementation of neoliberal fiscal and economic policies, then the rich will benefit. Warren Buffett (the richest man in the world in 2001) expressed this succinctly when he said: "Actually, there's been class warfare going on for the last 20 years, and my class has won. We're the ones that have gotten our tax rates reduced."[9]

The social mechanism that is indisputably the most crucial to a country's productivity and economic growth is the development, dissemination, and sharing of knowledge, says Piketty (2014: 21). This knowledge is embodied in new technology and innovation. Economic equality is also promoted by people's knowledge development (Atkinson & Piketty, 2010). This should indicate that knowledge development is the path to economic equality. However, since the 1980s, physical property, capital, and finance, as well as senior executives in large companies, have taken an ever-increasing share of the value creation. This has happened to the detriment of the wage share of knowledge workers, among others (Piketty, 2014: 21). On the other hand, we have witnessed the emergence of a high-income salaried elite who benefit greatly from their knowledge and competence. There is also a large group of wage earners who have seen their relative income fall (Jones, 2015; Weeks, 2014). The theoretical point being made here is that, over the last 40 years, financial capital has won over human capital; that is, capital income has increased at the expense of wage income.

Thus, since the 1980s and up until today, capital income's share of value creation has increased. The same has been the case for economic inequality (Piketty, 2014: 23–27). The factors that have contributed to greater economic inequality are the accumulation of wealth through property, financial income, and inheritance. This has occurred despite economic growth, which, according to Kuznets' theories, should lead to greater economic equality. It may also be said that this economic inequality has grown due to deliberate political policies (Piketty, 2014: 26–27).

Consequently, it is not the fact that capitalism has become sick that can explain the rise in inequality; it is rather that capitalism has never been as healthy as it is now. Healthy capitalism leads to economic inequality. Sick capitalism leads to fascism and totalitarian structures, economic crises, and war.

Sub-conclusion

The question we have investigated is: why does extreme economic inequality exist?

The short answer is that it is the result of deliberate political choices. The force that has driven greater economic equality is access to education, which has led to knowledge development, dissemination, transfer, and application.

Since neoliberalism broke through with Reagan and Thatcher in the 1980s, economic inequality has risen sharply in the West. Openness and free trade have led to some countries and companies benefitting, while others have suffered. For instance, the Chinese working and middle classes have largely benefitted from free trade, while the European and American working and middle classes have largely lost out. On the other hand, the rich have profited greatly from free trade. This has had political consequences, such as the drive to accelerate technological innovation with a focus on robotization.

The globalization that started around 2000 has changed the rules of the game for both economics and politics. The most important change in these rules of play is that national policies have become less important, while global forces are playing an ever-increasing role. One of the consequences is that the plutocracy is taking more control over the premises of economic development.

Sustaining social mechanisms

The question we investigate in this section is: what social mechanisms are sustaining extreme economic inequality?

We will describe, analyze, and discuss the following three social mechanisms: (1) the free market, (2) the ideology propagated by the men in suits, and (3) social and economic exclusion. For pedagogical reasons, we choose to describe, analyze, and discuss these three social mechanisms together.

Description

Among the assumptions that sustain economic inequality is the idea that it benefits everyone and is therefore necessary (Dorling, 2015: 37–99). However, this and other assumptions linked to economic inequality are not empirically documented; yet, they are propagated because they have become part of a belief system on par with other belief systems (Krugman, 2007; Galbraith, 1989: 260; Weeks, 2014: 1–19). "Greed is good," says Gordon Gekko in the film *Wall Street*. This catchphrase has become a maxim of the extremely rich, and is maintained by their intellectual henchmen (Bauman, 2007, 2013).

The belief that the market is free and beneficial to all represents an ideology that is espoused by the 'men in suits' – the intellectual henchmen who defend the necessity of inequality. This ideology leads to some people being socially and economically included, while others are excluded. Adam Smith was clearly aware of the negative consequences of a 'free' market when he said that for every very rich person there will be 500 poor.[10] Today (like in the 1700s), there is an admiration of the super-rich almost to the point of worship. This also contributes to reinforcing the perception of the free market as a prerequisite for economic prosperity for all, not just for the super-rich. The poor and the socially excluded are thus considered as something that has to be accepted if economic growth is desired. However, it is no more than a myth for which there exists no validating evidence (Krugman, 2007; Bauman, 2013). In the early stages of industrialization, Adam Smith expressed in his *Theory of Moral Sentiments* (1759) that this constituted the greatest distortion and corruption of our moral perception.[11]

In 2000, 10% of the world's population owned 85% of the world's wealth (Weeks, 2014). With globalization, this inequality has only increased in strength (Atkinson & Piketty, 2010). Today, 80% of the world's wealth is owned by the top 1% (Bauman, 2013); that is, 99% of the world's population owns 20% of the world's wealth.

The men in suits often claim that the poor have only themselves to blame for their poverty. They are stereotyped as being lazy, work-shy parasites living on welfare and unable to show any initiative. The number of clichés, stereotypes, and prejudices designed to keep the poor at the bottom and broke are endless. You even have sayings describing why some people are excluded while others are included, such as 'everyone is the architect of their own success.' The saying is of course a myth – but like all myths, it contains a little truth.

One of the ideas promoted by the men in suits is that what profits the individual is good for society as a whole. The pursuit of profit is thus supported by this generally accepted idea. The men in suits are committed to getting most of the 99% to believe that extreme inequality benefits everybody.

When people's standard of living steadily increases, large economic inequalities are not viewed as problematic. In addition, people have become socialized into the idea that when the rich get richer, everyone benefits. In this way, opposition to extreme economic inequality is hindered.

However, when economic growth stops, when uncertainty increases and people have problems finding full-time jobs that they can live off, then many feel they are being socially excluded. Such recent developments have led to the emergence of new groupings in society which Standing calls the "precariat" (Standing, 2014) and Shipler calls the "working poor" (Shipler, 2005). In recent years, inequality and uncertainty have been increasing for continually more people. The greater the distance between the economically excluded and the upper classes, the greater the likelihood that the precariat will rebel against such developments, says Standing (2014). Therefore, it is not unlikely that the super-rich and their intellectual henchmen will propose a 'citizen salary' in the future.

The idea that a rising tide lifts all boats which the men in suits try to sell in order to sustain their neoliberal ideology is also related to trickle-down economics.[12] The Norwegian proverb "When it rains on the priest, the sexton also gets wet" may also be said to illustrate trickle-down economics. In plain English, the idea is that if the wealthy are allowed to become wealthier, we will all benefit.

Analysis and discussion

The men in suits and the ideology they advocate obscures even the simplest relationships. This obscuring is not done because they have insight into the correct relationships, but rather because they have no idea about the relationships, says Weeks (2014: xiii). For instance, they put forward the claim of trickle-down economics as if it were a fact. The truth is rather that there is not a shred of empirical evidence that indicates that their claim is correct (Galbraith, 1989: 260). The assertion is essentially based on a lot of misleading, deceptive, and inconsistent theory that has not been shown to be empirically valid (Weeks, 2014: 1–19). On the other hand, it is easy to understand why those who profit from the spreading of these claims also pay handsomely for the service done on their behalf. Yet what is more difficult to understand is why so many people consider this ideology valid and correct. The simple answer is that propaganda is often effective, and more propaganda is more effective. So old wine is put into new bottles and people swallow it down as if it were new. Thus, when they have little knowledge of history, they are not only fooled once, but every time. When those who are served by the spreading of this ideology also own the media, it is not so difficult to understand why people occasionally drink old wine thinking it is new.

Perfect competition in a free market is the basis of the current neoliberal ideology, which must not however be confused with theory. On the other hand, the ideology is cloaked in an elaborate mathematical wrapper and presented as theory (Galbraith, 1989: 260). People's faith in the analyses of neoliberal economists may be partly explained by the man in the street's bewilderment of maths. However, it is important here to distinguish between mathematical theory and economic theory. When mathematical theory is applied to the economy, economic relationships do not necessarily become clearer, but rather veiled and difficult for most people to understand (Weeks, 2014: xv; Galbraith, 1989: 260). In this context, typical of obscuring beliefs is that the government receives most of its tax income from the private sector. The consequences of this type of thinking are that we must have a strong private sector if we want a strong welfare state. Of course, this claim serves the interests of the super-rich and is propagated by the men in suits. The truth is rather that the public sector contributes significantly to value creation in any society (Solow, 1956; Galbraith, 1989; Stiglitz, 2012; Bauman, 2013; Piketty, 2015; Krugman, 2007).

Banalities are presented as if they represented expertise and theoretical insight. However, they are only thinly disguised ideology and propaganda designed to profit the 1%. For instance, consider the following three:

1   Competition increases efficiency.
2   Privatization improves quality.
3   Freedom of choice is a prerequisite for freedom.

The men in suits have been extremely active in spreading such banalities as if they represented some kind of staggering insights. This is done to take control of public opinion, politics, culture, and social systems.

The whole mode of thinking concerning competition, privatization, and freedom of choice constitutes nothing more than paying lip service to the rich. The executive leaders who reap the benefits of neoliberal policies are very well paid. It is no coincidence that executive salaries have risen sharply since the 1980s, when the neoliberal policies were rapidly introduced, and the three clichés listed above started to reverberate throughout political systems. Later, neoliberal ideas would invade every nook and crook of the economic, social, cultural, and political systems.

Generally speaking, competition is a struggle or test of strength between two or more parties to get or win something that the other also wants.[13] A slightly different definition is a situation where someone tries to win something or achieve success at the expense of others.[14]

For economists, however, competition does not involve a process as described above but is rather related to results. Furthermore, in their conceptual world, there is a win-win situation for the total system (Weeks, 2014: 19). Nevertheless, in business, similar to competitive sports, there are those who win and those who lose. The losing party does not improve by losing.

Market share is an indicator of how well a company is doing compared to others. However, a larger market share will also mean a smaller market share for others and consequently a reduction in consumer choice. This mechanism pushes prices down but also pushes down wages and can lead to outsourcing to low-cost countries. In this competitive process, many businesses are also pushed out of the market, resulting in profit increases for the few remaining. The paradox is that when more competitors are pushed out of the market, prices will then rise and profits will increase further for the few remaining. This process reinforces the extreme economic inequality we are witnessing today.

The belief in perfect competition in a free market is precisely that: a belief, in line with believing in elves, trolls, and elemental beings. Neither does the 'free' market create, as it is claimed, 'free' people. It may create freedom in one sense – freedom for the few to become extremely rich (Piketty, 2014). When the men in suits attempt to counter this criticism, they argue that there are certain conditions that must be fulfilled for free competition to exist. This is correct. Theoretically, six conditions need to be fulfilled to ensure free competition.[15] However, this theory only remains on the theoretical level in the sense that it cannot be applied to the real world, at least not to the global economy. None of the six conditions is fulfilled in the global competitive economy (Weeks, 2014). Consequently, the theory of free competition is completely detached from practice; neither is the theory of any help in trying to understand what happens in practice. This also applies despite the fact that theory concerning free competition is often backed up by using mathematical formulas that only the 'priests' of economy are able to fathom.

Although mathematical formulas are often used to support the merits of competition, there is no valid analytical economic theory that supports such calculations (Weeks, 2014: 22). The consequence is that 'free competition' remains an empty concept with no more content than that of mathematical rhetoric. However, the mathematical rhetoric has a clear purpose: it enables the rich to become even richer, and this is precisely what has happened from the 1980s up until today.

The proponents of free competition in a free market often start with a single example and then they develop arguments based on the example; thus, they generalize from a single case. This reasoning may be said to be on the same level as saying that the chicken came before the egg, because I have a chicken and I can see that it lays eggs. Any ten-year-old knows that the next question will be "where does the chicken come from?" The proponents of free competition and the free market go no further than their single example, and then they formulate mathematical 'evidence' to support the example, which they seemingly believe solves the problem of the chicken and the egg, or free competition and the so-called free market.

Markets have existed for thousands of years. There is nothing wrong with markets as such. It is rather the idea of building a theory of society around so-called free competition in free markets that is harmful. It is harmful because it has negative social and economic consequences for many people. It leads to social inclusion for some, but social exclusion for many (Standing, 2014; Shipler, 2005). A market involves commercial dealings where people interact by buying, selling, and exchanging goods and services and entering into agreements. The market is not something that was invented during industrialization, or by the men in suits.

The idea that anyone can get rich in a free market economy is a deeply entrenched myth. This myth sustains economic inequality, because everyone imagines that they can be the one that gets rich. Although only a few can become rich, the myth is that anyone can become one of the few. It is just a case of having the right ideas, passion, persistence, self-discipline, and a desire to create something new (Duckworth, 2017).[16] Thus, the hero of the myth is not born rich but starts with only two empty hands. However, in the real global economy, the majority of those who have become richer are those who were rich in the first place (Atkinson & Piketty, 2010; Piketty, 2014, 2015). Of course, there are always exceptions – a few may have managed to become super-rich by starting with two empty hands, and it is these few who are made into examples of how you can get rich. Yet, these few contrast starkly with the millions that never get rich, but who live in uncertainty (Standing, 2014; Jones, 2015).

From the 1980s up until today, the political authorities, well assisted by the men in suits, have made society into a money machine for the extremely rich. They have reduced tax on capital income, and also reduced and in part eliminated inheritance taxes, so that extreme wealth is inherited, thus freezing social inequalities. Wealth is also inherited in other ways. There is a close relationship between parental income and children's school achievements, which is an important social mechanism for success (OECD, 2012). For instance, it is less likely that the children of single mothers on welfare support will do well at school compared to the children of the well-off.[17] The truth is that the majority of the poor remain poor, and the majority of the rich remain rich, although there are of course, as mentioned, exceptions (Jones, 2015).

Sub-conclusion

The question we have examined in this section is the following: what social mechanisms are sustaining extreme economic inequality? The short answer is that the free market, the men in suits, free competition, and free trade sustain economic inequality. We have shown this in Figure 3.2.

The alternative to free markets, free competition, and free trade is not five-year plans and central planning. The alternative is competition directed towards shared

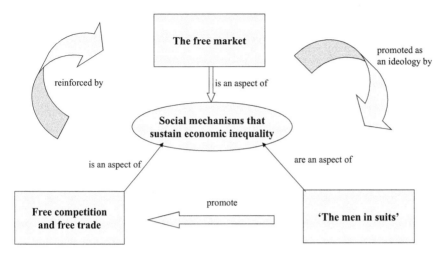

Figure 3.2 Social mechanisms that sustain economic inequality

prosperity, cooperation and mutual trade agreements based on historical developments, context, industry, and situation.

The justification of equality

The question we investigate in this section is: why is economic equality preferable?

To explain the justification of equality, we will describe and analyze two factors: perceived justice and perceived welfare. These factors are systemic and will therefore be considered together in the description, analysis, and discussion.

Description

Fighting for greater economic equality has traditionally been the domain of left-wing politicians and activists. However in 2015, two liberal institutions, the OECD and IMF, published studies that concluded that economic inequality could hinder economic growth.[18] The men in suits were quick to discredit the methodology used in the reports.[19] First, there is of course no clear connection between economic equality and economic growth. Second, neither is there a clear connection between economic inequality and economic growth. Yet, the latter (a positive connection between economic inequality and economic growth) has always been supported by the men in suits, while few of the 'wise men of economics' have argued against this belief in the media. However, when reports were published showing that economic equality can lead to economic growth, these wise men of economics were quick to point out the methodological problems. One might wonder why.

However, economic equality does not need to postulate economic growth as an argument. The prime argument for economic equality is perceived justice and fairness, and that economic inequality creates an unjust society.[20] Economic inequality in general, and extreme economic inequality in particular, results in the few becoming 'free,' while others become unfree. Economic inequality and especially extreme economic inequality result in the freedom of the few, yet the devaluation and exclusion of many others.

Jost (2012) makes the point that economic equality motivates commitment and creativity. Just as great economic inequality results in social exclusion, economic equality results in social inclusion (Milanovic, 2016). Privileges, elites, and inequality create tensions and conflicts, which reduce value creation (Chomsky, 2017; Piketty, 2015).

There are many factors that can explain why people do not oppose extreme economic inequality, despite the realization that inequality inhibits creativity and commitment. One of the factors is the idea that economic inequality is considered to be a 'law of nature.' You often hear expressions of the type that: 'this is the way it's always been.' However, this is a fallacious belief; it hasn't 'always been like this' (Sahlin, 2017). On the contrary, history shows us that it is possible to do something about economic injustice (Sahlin, 2017a). For instance, in the Scandinavian countries, economic inequality measured by the Gini coefficient is relatively small.[21] However, if one believes something is a law of nature, then one resigns and chooses to accept something as inevitable.

Analysis and discussion

It is a paradox that those who experience the greatest economic injustice are those who do not act against it to any large degree. This may be explained by society's and the various systems' justification of the benefits of inequality to everybody, which is accepted by most people, but most of all by those who earn the least (Jost, 2012). To exaggerate the point, one might even say that those who are most negatively affected by economic inequality are those who accept the premises of the inequality, more so than those who are not affected to such a degree. Furthermore, empirical research shows that those who earn the least, have the worst jobs, and are uncertain of their economic future, are those who mostly accept the state of things (Jost et al., 2003). Thus those who have the lowest wages largely accept the necessity of economic inequality (Jost et al., 2003). Similar tendencies are suggested by the prospect theory of Kahneman & Tversky (1979, 2000), which states that you spend more energy on preventing loss than fighting for something better than you have.

It may seem that the acceptance of the necessity of economic inequality is a form of political pain medication. One accepts the negative effects of economic inequality because the pain of accepting economic inequality is less than doing something about it. It may also be the case that those who are most negatively affected accept the economic inequality because they are socially included in something larger than themselves; this may also give them the hope and belief that economic inequality can lead to those who have little improving their lives. It is precisely this myth that the upper class has effectively managed to sell to those who experience the negative consequences of economic inequality. The theoretical point being made here is that people rationalize their own situation and give legitimacy to the state of things. The practical utility in this context, from this insight, is that the more the upper class argues that everyone profits from economic inequality, the more this argument is accepted by those who are the victims of the inequality.

It is these social mechanisms that maintain the economic wall of inequality, which allows some to live in extreme prosperity, while others experience economic uncertainty on the other side of the economic wall. The mortar that holds the wall together are the social mechanisms that allow those who are negatively affected by economic inequality to accept the state of things, because they feel it represents a natural state of affairs.

If the mortar loses its cohesive force, then the wall of economic inequality will fall down. The social mechanisms are no more than perceptions, beliefs, and surmises. There is no empirical evidence that necessitates sustaining extreme economic inequality. This leads us to the question: what promotes economic value creation?

There is a negative relationship between tax cuts for the rich and the prosperity of the majority (Bauman, 2013; Stiglitz, 2015; Piketty, 2014, 2015). Extreme economic inequality also creates social barriers that inhibit social relationships across the economic wall. Regardless of one's view concerning economic growth, to a certain extent it has led to improved welfare and health and longer life (Wilkinson & Pickett, 2010: 3–14).

Extreme economic inequality expresses itself in relationships between people. In Western countries, poverty is often defined as earning less than 60% of the average income. Thus, it does not necessarily mean that one is dressed in rags or suffers from lack of shelter or hunger. On the other hand, it does correlate to poorer health, shorter life expectancy, poorer coping ability, and a standard of life that could be better in many ways (Shipler, 2005). Poverty is linked to relationships, status, position, illness, early death, and often lack of participation in community life (Standing, 2014).

As a rule, statistics show that countries with the greatest economic growth are also those countries where economic inequality is lowest. The theoretical point is that economic growth and economic equality are positively related, which has been shown by many, including Stiglitz (2002, 2012) and Piketty (2015). Furthermore, empirical data shows that the countries with the highest levels of economic equality are those countries where there is greater trust between people, fewer mental disorders, longer life expectancy, lower levels of malnutrition, higher levels of education, fewer suicides, smaller prison populations, fewer social and health problems, and greater social mobility (Wilkinson & Pickett, 2010: 19–30).

Economic inequality teaches us to place others in the social hierarchy, and then we relate to this hierarchy (Sahlin, 2013, 2017). In countries where capital income is high in relation to wage income, there are also greater economic differences (Piketty, 2015).

In Denmark, where economic inequality is not that great, it takes an average senior executive five days to earn the annual salary of an industry worker.[22] In Norway, which is also one of the most egalitarian countries in the world, we can read the following in the conservative Norwegian newspaper *Aftenposten*: "One in ten children in Norway are now growing up in poverty."[23] Such extreme inequalities have far-ranging economic, social, cultural, and political consequences.

No empirical evidence can show that the higher the salaries executives receive, the better they perform their jobs. It is the notion that the high salaries received by executives are in everyone's interests that maintains inequality (Jost, 2012; Jost et al., 2003). It is also a fallacious idea that in those societies where economic inequality is the greatest, effectiveness is greater than in egalitarian societies (Piketty, 2014, 2016). It is also erroneous to believe that societies sort out the best to become leaders (Sahlin, 2017a). It is also incorrect to argue that our social system is merely a reflection of nature's social organization. It is rather the case that for more than 90% of human history, people have lived in hunting and gathering cultures, which were not characterized by economic inequality (although some may obviously have been more skilled than others) (Boehm, 2012). Societies characterized by great inequalities only started to appear in human history at what may be likened to the blink of an eye (Sahlin, 2017, 2017a).

However, one can understand why the upper class and their ideological henchmen, the men in suits, make the comparison with nature. By such a comparison, inequality is presented as a law of nature, which it is not. Comparison with nature has a clear purpose: to support and reinforce economic inequality. It is always the position of the privileged that such assumptions are designed to sustain. The theoretical point is that economic inequality is not a prerequisite for the prosperity of the many. The practical utility of this point is that people's actions and willingness to do something about inequality will be activated.

If we consider others as potential competitors, we will create one type of society. If we consider others as potential partners, and try to help them to meet their needs, we will create a qualitatively different society.

The dominance logic of the wolf pack develops social layers with relatively closed barriers between the layers. The logic of cooperation develops cohesive power, creating a community that gives meaning (Grant, 2014). Economic equality and the development of prosperity are linked to sharing, giving, cooperating, and understanding mutuality (Grant, 2016; Piketty, 2014, 2016). If we see the wolf in others, then we meet them with our teeth bared. If we see the others as partners, we meet them with respect, responsibility, and dignity (Sahlin, 2013).

Sub-conclusion

The question we have examined in this section is: why is economic equality preferable? We have described, analyzed, and discussed two factors: perceived justice and perceived welfare. These factors are systemic and are shown in Figure 3.3.

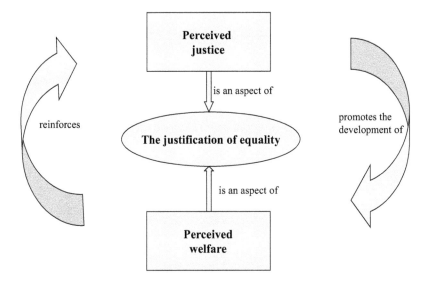

Figure 3.3 The justification of equality

Main conclusion

This chapter has explored the following question:

WHAT IS PROMOTING EXTREME ECONOMIC INEQUALITY?

The following four factors are promoting extreme economic inequality:

1   The free market
2   The ideology disseminated by the men in suits
3   Free trade
4   Free competition.

In this concluding section, we have opted to respond to the aforementioned question by indicating policy measures that may promote economic equality. We have done so because measures that may promote greater economic equality are linked directly to factors that promote extreme economic inequality.

We know from various sources that economic security, friendship, and collaboration promote health and welfare. We know also that longevity and wellness among those at the bottom of the economic ladder are worse than among those higher up. We know also that extreme economic inequality fosters distrust, overcrowded prisons, violence, criminality, and urban unrest.

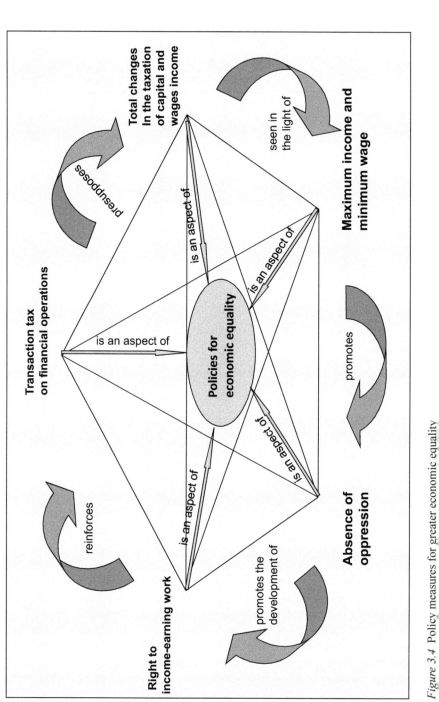

Figure 3.4 Policy measures for greater economic equality

There has been an extreme change in the relationship between unearned and earned income, favouring people with capital investments. This change started around 1980 with the growth of neoliberalism. It gathered pace with the advent of globalization approximately from the start of the 21st century. However, several interventions could reverse this trend. One proposal that has been suggested is the so-called Tobin tax, which is a type of transaction tax on financial operations.[24] A second measure could be to tax unearned income at much higher rates and to reduce tax rates for people on low and average incomes. A third, more radical approach would be to introduce both a minimum wage and a maximum income, with both earned and unearned income forming the basis of calculations. A maximum income could be implemented quite easily, for instance, by imposing a limit on income of five times the average salary. All income above that level would be taxed at 100%. This kind of arrangement would be effective in preventing the trend we are witnessing today, with the wealthiest 1% becoming even richer.

We also have a non-economic factor that could help promote greater economic equality. This is freedom from oppression. Being subjected to oppression can have major negative economic consequences. The final suggestion is that the right to income-earning work should be a right based in law. This could be envisaged as an obligation of the state and a human right equivalent to the obligation of the state to provide education. We have purposely excluded a citizen salary from our proposed policy, because a citizen salary would probably act as a social mechanism maintaining social inequality.

Notes

1 https://en.wikipedia.org/wiki/Robert_Mundell, accessed 26 March 2017.
2 www.investopedia.com/articles/05/011805.asp, accessed 26 March 2017.
3 http://democracyjournal.org/magazine/29/burying-supply-side-once-and-for-all/, accessed 26 March 2017.
4 http://democracyjournal.org/magazine/29/burying-supply-side-once-and-for-all/, accessed 26 March 2017.
5 Robert Solow won the Nobel Prize for Economics in 1987; https://da.wikipedia.org/wiki/Robert_Solow.
6 Informats are robots that are in contact with each other and with information and knowledge online.
7 DN.no, 15 April 2017, accessed 15 April 2017.
8 The classical economists are Thomas Malthus, David Ricardo and Adam Smith.
9 G. Sargent cited Buffett in the *Washington Post*, 30 September 2011.
10 Adam Smith cited in Bauman (2013: 1).
11 Adam Smith cited in Bauman (2013: 1).
12 https://en.wikipedia.org/wiki/Trickle-down_economics.
13 Webster's dictionary.
14 Cambridge dictionary.
15 The six conditions are as follows. (1) There are many businesses, each of which has a relatively small market share. (2) Each business has similar output. (3) Consumers are given complete information about prices and suppliers. (4) All the businesses have equal access to resources. (5) There are no barriers to entry into the market or to leave the market. (6) There are no externalities that affect the market. This means, among other things, that there will be no innovations.
16 Duckworth (2017) calls this GRIT.

17 The Danish newspaper, *Politiken*, 11 May 2017.
18 The Danish newspaper, *Information*, 10 May 2017.
19 The Danish 'wise men of economics' were critical of the studies. In an article in the newspaper *Berlingske* (8 May 2017), the methodological arguments used to demonstrate the causal relationship between economic equality and economic growth were judged as being problematic. Professor of Economics Carl-Johan Dalgaard (University of Copenhagen) followed up in the newspaper *Information* (9 May 2017) using similar argumentation.
20 *Information*, 10 May 2017.
21 https://no.wikipedia.org/wiki/Gini-koeffisient.
22 *Information*, 27 March 2017.
23 The Norwegian newspaper, *Aftenposten*, 17 March 2017.
24 https://en.wikipedia.org/wiki/Tobin_tax.

References

Atkinson, A. & Piketty, T. (2010). *Top income: A global perspective*, Oxford University Press, Oxford.
Bauman, Z. (2007). *Consuming life*, Polity Press, Cambridge.
Bauman, Z. (2013). *Does the richness of the few benefit us all?*, Polity Press, New York.
Boehm, C. (2012). *Moral origins: The evolution of virtue, altruism and shame*, Basic Books, New York.
Chomsky, N. (2017). *Requiem for the American dream*, Seven Stories Press, New York.
Dorling, D. (2015). *Inequality and the 1%*, Verso, London.
Duckworth, A. (2017). *GRIT why passion and resilience are the secrets to success*, Vermilion, London.
Galbraith, J. G. (1989). *A history of economics: The past and the present*, Penguin, New York.
Grant, A. (2014). *Give and take, helping others drive our success*, W&N, New York.
Grant, A. (2016). *Originals*, WH Allen, New York.
Jones, O. (2015). *The establishment and how they get away with it*, Penguin Books, London.
Jost, J. T. (2012). Why men (and women) do and don't rebel: Effects on system justification and willingness to protest, *Personality and Social Psychology Bulletin*, 38:197–208.
Jost, J. T., Pelham, B. W., Sheldon, O. & Sullivan, B. (2003). Social inequality and the reduction of ideological dissonance on behalf of the system, *European Journal of Social Psychology*, 33:13–36.
Kahneman, D. & Tversky, A. (1979). An analysis of decision under risk, *Econometrica, Journal of the Econometric Society*, 47, 2:263–292.
Kahneman, D. & Tversky, A. (2000). Prospect theory: An analysis of decision under risk, in Kahneman, D. & Tversky, A. (Eds.). *Choices, values and frames*, Cambridge University Press, Cambridge, pp. 17–43.
Krugman, P. (2007). *The conscience of a liberal*, W. W. Norton, New York.
Kuznets, S. (1953). *Shares of upper income groups in income and savings*, National Bureau of Economic Research, Cambridge, MA.
Kuznets, S. (1955). Economic growth and income inequality, *American Economic Review*, 45, 1:1–28.
Mandel, E. (1964). *The economics of neo-capitalism*, The Socialist Register, Amsterdam.
Mandel, E. (1980). *Long waves of capitalist development: The Marxist interpretation*, Cambridge University Press, New York.

Milanovic, B. (2016). *Global inequality, a new approach for the age of globalization*, Belknap Press, Boston.

OECD. (2012). *Economic policy reforms: Going for growth*, Paris.

Piketty, T. (2014). *Capital in the twenty-first century*, Belknap Press, Boston.

Piketty, T. (2016). *The economics of inequality*, Belknap Press, Boston.

Sahlin, M. (2013). *What Kinship is*, University of Chicago Press, Chicago.

Sahlin, M. (2017). *Stone age economics*, Routledge, London.

Sahlin, M. (2017a). *Kings*, University of Chicago Press, Chicago.

Shipler, D. (2005). *The working poor*, Vintage, New York.

Solow, R. (1956). A contribution to the theory of economic growth, *Quarterly Journal of Economics*, 70, 1:65–94.

Standing, G. (2014). *The precariat: The new dangerous class*, Bloomsbury Academic, New York.

Stiglitz, J. (2002). *Globalization and its discontents*, W. W. Norton, New York.

Stiglitz, J. (2012). *The price of inequality*, Princeton, London.

Stiglitz, J. (2015). *The great divide*, Penguin, London.

Weeks, J. H. (2014). *Economics of the 1%*, Anthem Press, New York.

Wilkinson, R. & Pickett, K. (2010). *The spirit level: Why equality is better for everyone*, Penguin, New York.

Wolff, J. & De-Shalit, A. (2007). *Disadvantage*, Oxford University Press, Oxford.

Appendix

Historical account of the use of the term 'feudal capitalism'

Feudalism was the dominant social system in Medieval Europe. *Feodalis*, a Latin term that originates from the Middle Ages, means 'vassal' (i.e. a holder of land on the condition of allegiance and homage to a lord). *Feodum*, Latin for 'fiefdom,' was the land or estate owned by a lord. A fief was the main element of feudalism – a property held by a vassal who paid fealty to a lord in the form of allegiance, homage, and tribute. Tributes could be in the form of money, protection fees, or the like, but the respect shown was also important.[1] Feudal structures were so hated by the people that by the time of the French Revolution of 1789, one of the principal goals of the revolution was to completely abolish the feudal system (Block, 2014: xv).

Some reasons for the emergence of feudal society may be explained by the raids and robberies carried out by Muslims, Hungarians, and Vikings in Europe. It was a period of uncertainty, turbulence, and disorder. This led to the need for protection, predictability, and security for the population. The new system that emerged embodied feudal laws and more or less fixed social structures.

Feudal society was characterized by a framework of institutions. One of the institutions that developed in the Middle Ages was the city. They became larger and promoted the development of what Luhmann calls 'functional differentiation' (Luhmann, social system). Other elements that characterized feudal society were: a common language, Latin; a common belief, Catholicism; and a common enemy, the Muslims (Block, 2014: 5–94).

At the end of the 11th century and in the 12th century, there was an increasing interest in learning about the past. Epic, heroic poems were in fashion, and the Late Medieval period in the 14th century saw the beginnings of an intellectual renaissance. The rule of custom was prominent before law became more central. In the development of the latter, the laws of the Roman period were studied and Roman law became a concept. Through the law, hierarchical complex relationships were developed (Block, 2014: 94–130).

Kinship, clan, and family ties became important social mechanisms to protect interests in feudal society. Additional security was gained by the individual through becoming a vassal of a lord or king. Family ties also protected individuals in the courts. This meant that private vengeance and vendetta were features throughout the feudal period. Feuding between families was a widespread phenomenon. Feuding was thus institutionalized to the extent that it was led by a chieftain. Family ties were strengthened through marriage, ceremonies, and the law.

The institution of obedience cannot only be traced to the Church (Romans 13:1–7) but also through the submission of the vassal to his lord or king. This submission occurred through the ceremony of homage.[2] Homage is a very special institution that ensures obedience, duty, and faithfulness of the vassal to his lord or king. The vassal was *symbolic* of the hierarchical structures of the Middle Ages – the vassal was *the man of another man*, and characterizes the institution of subordination and obedience in feudal society (Block, 2014: 155). 'Homage' is thus a mutual relationship where the vassal submits to and serves his lord, but is also under the protection of his lord. This submission was often symbolized by the vassal kneeling down before his lord and then kissing the lord's hand as a sign of the establishment of the vassal-lord relationship. The vassal relationship was inherited, even though the ceremony had to be carried out for each relationship. In brief, the relationship between the vassal and his lord may be stated in one sentence: 'To serve and to protect.'

'Manorialism' was a widespread organizational form in feudal society. In short, the vassal leased a piece of land from his lord. This fief could then be used to provide for his family, but he had to pay a certain amount of money (interest) for the loan at set times of the year.[3]

Feudal society was characterized by a network of socially dependent relationships. The networks were like Russian dolls, one with greater power and influence than the other.

The nobility, the leading social class in feudal society, were the rich: those with power and position, the lords and their families. This was the aristocracy of the Middle Ages. They lived their lives separately from the underclass and their vassals. The class of vassals also included professional soldiers, the knights who were vassals to a lord but who also served the king or queen. Marriage within the nobility was a type of business transaction, linking families together.

The nobility eventually developed into a social class that was protected by the legislators. Similarly, the vassals and knights and their descendants were protected by law and formed a separate social class. They represented what we would call the upper part of the middle class today.

Distinctions were also developed within the nobility, some being placed higher than others. Those who stood closest to the king or queen were the highest ranking, and then distinctions were made downwards in this hierarchy dependent upon the relationship between the noble and the king or queen. Church leaders also constituted part of the nobility and were an important part of the social and economic power structure of feudal society.

Concurrent with the development of the social classes comprising the nobility and vassals was the development of a legal system. This system legalized the social structures and judged by law those who opposed it.

As power was accumulated within the social hierarchies, there was a need to make distinctions in relation to rulers and nations. Wars, empires, dynasties, and new alliances grew out of this. Territories were established, ruled over by lords and barons who built castles and forts to protect their newly acquired territories.

The feudal system as described here was a type of social system chronologically placed in the Middle Ages and unknown in earlier or later historical periods.

Notes

1 https://en.wikipedia.org/wiki/Tribute.
2 https://en.wikipedia.org/wiki/Homage_(feudal).
3 https://en.wikipedia.org/wiki/Manorialism.

Reference

Luhman, N. (1995). *Social systems*, Stanford University Press, Stanford.

Index

Note: Page numbers in italic indicate a figure on the corresponding page.

For Product Safety Concerns and Information please contact our EU
representative GPSR@taylorandfrancis.com
Taylor & Francis Verlag GmbH, Kaufingerstraße 24, 80331 München, Germany

www.ingramcontent.com/pod-product-compliance
Ingram Content Group UK Ltd.
Pitfield, Milton Keynes, MK11 3LW, UK
UKHW021825240425
457818UK00006B/78